THE POLITICS OF CRISIS

An Insider's Prescription to Prevent Public Policy Disasters

ERIC KOWALCZYK

INDIE BOOKS
INTERNATIONAL

No part of this publication may be reproduced or distributed in any form or by any means without the prior permission of the publisher. Requests for permission should be directed to permissions@indiebooksintl.com, or mailed to Permissions, Indie Books International, 2424 Vista Way, Suite 316, Oceanside, CA 92054.

Neither the publisher nor the author is engaged in rendering legal or other professional services through this book. If expert assistance is required, the services of appropriate professionals should be sought. The publisher and the author shall have neither liability nor responsibility to any person or entity with respect to any loss or damage caused directly or indirectly by the information in this publication.

ISBN-10: 1-947480-41-3
ISBN-13: 978-1-947480-41-4
Library of Congress Control Number: 2018965529

Designed by Joni McPherson, www.mcphersongraphics.com

To the women and men of the Baltimore Police Department who serve today, and in days gone by, with honor, integrity, and morality.

CONTENTS

Preface vii

Chapter 1: The Day That Changed My Life. 1

Chapter 2: How We Got Here 9

Chapter 3: Homicides Drive Policing 19

Chapter 4: A New Police Commissioner, a New Day 31

Chapter 5: Exposing the Truth 39

Chapter 6: A City on the Brink of Disaster 49

Chapter 7: Eyes Wide Shut. 55

Chapter 8: This Is Our Ferguson 61

Chapter 9: The National Media Arrives. 69

Chapter 10: Violence Rocks Baltimore 75

Chapter 11: The Prelude to More Violence 87

Chapter 12: The Riot Seen around the World 93

Chapter 13: Baltimore Burns 107

Chapter 14: The Waves Keep Crashing 117

Chapter 15: Time to Leave. 125

Chapter 16: Crushing Darkness 137

Chapter 17: Taking Stock of the Present 145

Chapter 18: A Different Vision. 153

Chapter 19: A New Direction. 161

Acknowledgments 167

About the Author 169

Works Referenced 171

PREFACE

Perception.

Perception is everything. It defines the way we see the world. It shapes our experiences. It creates our memories, and everyone's perception is different. We hear so often how important perception is. Yet, when it comes down to it, we really don't spend a whole lot of time thinking about it. We go about our daily existence, content in our routines, worried about bills that need to be paid, hopeful for vacations we have yet to take. We love our jobs or hate them. Love our spouses or hate them. We plod through life and, while each one of us is unique, our existence is remarkably similar.

We make hundreds of decisions a day. What time to wake up, what toothpaste to use, what to have for breakfast. We don't think of these as life-defining moments. Yet any one of a hundred decisions we make has the potential to be that life-defining moment of change. And therein lies the rub. The mundane can become the extraordinary. That one seemingly minor decision affects the course of your life. Sometimes that decision can affect the lives of tens of thousands of people. And they will all look at the decision you made through their own perceptions.

Police officers make an incalculable number of decisions each day. I know; I spent more than a decade making those decisions. Whom to arrest, whom not to arrest. Which car to stop, which to let go. I never really thought about the impact of those decisions at the time I made them. The moment appeared and I decided. Simple as that. Only very rarely are the decisions police officers make simple. More often than not, we affect the lives of everyone we encounter for good or for bad.

When one of those decisions we make affects a person negatively, it can spiral. That interaction can reach a family, a neighborhood, a community, a city, or an entire nation. On April 12, 2015, a few Baltimore City Police officers made what at the time seemed like an inconsequential decision. They arrested a man in West Baltimore—something that happens more times in a week than the average person can even comprehend. They never thought, at the moment the handcuffs were placed on Freddie Gray, a series of events would transpire that would shape the future of the City of Baltimore, the law enforcement profession, and the lives of untold thousands.

Each person has his or her own perception of what took place in Baltimore during the months of April and May of 2015. Shaped by unique life experiences, those perceptions are powerful. To live through a riot, media chaos, and political intrigue is a life-altering experience. Those experiences changed my life in ways that I could not have imagined. The events of that time helped me to see the critical need for law enforcement, as a profession, to change in fundamental ways. I heard the human cry borne of years of systemic oppression, racism, and violence. I saw a community and a police department ripped apart. My experience also galvanized demons I was wrestling with regarding the conduct of my own career and my department.

Not everyone will agree with me or my perceptions. I hope to change those minds. I hope my experiences can play a small role in helping the next generation of police officers do a better job of being partners and problem-solvers in their community.

This is my story.

Eric Kowalczyk
Baltimore, October 2018

CHAPTER 1

The Day That Changed My Life

It is not the critic who counts; not the man who points out how the strong man stumbles, or where the doer of deeds could have done them better.

The credit belongs to the man who is actually in the arena.

—TEDDY ROOSEVELT

The morning of April 12, 2015, was like any other Sunday. I was in bed at 9:24 a.m., curled up next to my boyfriend, Jeff, when the phone rang. It was Colonel Garnell Green, the head of our Office of Internal Oversight, calling to tell me that we had a prisoner with a broken neck, that it was as serious as it could get, and that I shouldn't worry—he had done it to himself. I was assured that we had a witness statement corroborating what I had just been told. I was groggy, tired, and warm. I was in bed; I didn't want to wake up. I did not fully comprehend what I was being told. I had no idea that phone call would lead to thirty days of chaos as the world turned its eyes to Baltimore and we learned that the life and death of Freddie Gray would change the course of history in the city forever.

I had become the chief spokesman of the Baltimore Police Department on June 26, 2013. At the time, I was a sergeant about to be promoted to lieutenant. I had no formal media training, no experience in public relations, no idea how to formulate media strategy or shape a message. I was brought down to then-Public Affairs because of my ability to work with community groups. I had a passion for it, I believed in it, and I was good at it. Public messaging and media messaging needed to be combined, and I was the lynchpin. The director at the time was talented and skilled, and I learned a tremendous amount under his leadership. He also deeply disagreed with the direction the department was moving in, and after an interview in which he made a comment that was construed by some as being dismissive of a wave of crippling violence, he was replaced. By me.

A brilliant communicator named Judy Pal trained me. A fiery redhead, she could hang with the boys and had no trouble telling it like it was; she could message the hell out of any situation. Her slight stature was betrayed by a booming personality that could keep the good ol' boys in check and bring salty police to silence. I didn't know it at the time, but working and learning by her side through scandal after scandal in 2013 would prepare me better than any course, any institution, or any university ever could have. I soaked up every lesson she had to teach, ready to represent 3,000 men and women who comprised the eighth-largest police department in the nation.

Judy came to the department with more than thirty years of experience. In her role as chief of staff for the department, she was helping the new commissioner institute necessary reforms. She had a reputation as a problem-solver. Departments in need of reform would bring her in and tap into her brilliant mind to effect needed change. She had worked her magic in Atlanta, Savannah, Halifax, and Milwaukee. Her core focus was on transparency, integrity, and pushing decision-making down through the organization in an effort to empower people at every level of responsibility to rise to the challenge. She would become a friend, a mentor, a confidant, and a sounding board in the most challenging moment of my life.

From June 2013 to March 2015, my team worked every day to push the boundaries of what it meant to be in media relations. We stopped playing favorites with one reporter, opened dialogue with all our media partners, and worked to repair decades of damage in the community. We tapped into the power of social media, pushing the boundaries of what was "acceptable" for a police department. From videos of officers dancing to cutting-edge recruiting videos, we built our Twitter following from 28,000 to nearly 80,000 by March 2015. The power of social media to shape mainstream media was clear, and we used every opportunity to drive stories. The effort was never about public relations stunts. Instead, we focused on catering content to the people of Baltimore. We tried to strike a balance between real crime information and inside looks at the department. Every week we would highlight a different unit in the agency. Videos and Twitter town halls were our way of opening the department up to the community. Social media interaction was a technique that would serve us well in the coming days.

My experience during the riots did not take place in a vacuum. I had a dedicated, selfless team that sacrificed all to give of themselves for the department. And during the days of the riots, people whose names will never be known cleaned tables and carpets so that officers would have a clean place to rest for a few moments. Commanders gave parts of their souls as they watched their officers hold the line, bleeding and battered, protecting the people who were spitting at them, hurting them, calling them murderers. During the Battle of Mondawmin and the defense of Baltimore, many people played roles that were far more dangerous than mine. My task was to define for the world what we were doing. It was to add context to a tragedy that should never have happened. I defended a police commissioner who, for a love of the integrity of the badge, fought to hold a city together and forever change the face of law enforcement.

—•—

I had been in the Headquarters Annex Building elevator hundreds of times, from my office on the first floor to the police commissioner's office on the fifth and back. I knew every movement and sound of the elevator car. I could time the ride without even thinking about it. Today, it didn't have the same comforting feeling I was accustomed to. Today, the elevator felt like a cage, hurling me toward a future I didn't want to face. As the elevator doors opened, I couldn't help thinking, "This isn't supposed to be me." It was a mantra that thrummed its incessant beat.

How in the hell did I end up in this position? It was April 27, 2015, and I was about to hold what would arguably be the most important media briefing of my life. As the captain/director of media relations for the Baltimore Police Department (BPD), I was the one who had to explain to a global audience why Baltimore was on fire. Why were seemingly thousands of people across East and West Baltimore engaged in the first riot the city had witnessed in forty years?

I had watched, along with the rest of the nation, the media coverage of the riots in Ferguson, Missouri. I knew how national and global networks had picked apart every word that was uttered by government officials during that crisis. I knew that what I said in the next five minutes would set the tone for how the ensuing events would be covered. I knew that law enforcement analysts would examine every word I said as well as how I said them.

I knew I would be translated into Russian, Japanese, German, and every other language spoken by the hordes of media from around the world that had descended on Baltimore.

More important to me was what the people of Baltimore would think. This was our city. It was in pain. It was in crisis. And now, it was on fire. As the sound of my footsteps echoed through an oddly and ominously quiet lobby, I again questioned how I was the person who was doing this. I had never sought to be the chief spokesperson for the BPD. This had never been envisioned as my career path, and I was worried that I wouldn't live up to the demands of the moment. That I would say the wrong thing and let down my agency, dishonor the police officers who at that very moment were being assaulted with rocks and bricks. That in my desire to differentiate between the peaceful protests of the previous few weeks and the horror we were witnessing now, I would say something that made the friends and family of Freddie Gray feel as if we didn't care about their grief. I worried I would say something that could be used to incite more rioters. That I would give credence to the provocateurs of destruction, bent on tearing down the fragile peace we had maintained for the last week.

And then it was time.

I walked out onto the bricks in front of headquarters. Standing in front of our memorial wall of those who had been killed in the line of duty, I looked at more cameras than I could count. A bank of microphones and what looked like a rat's nest of lavalier microphones were waiting for me in the center of the media scrum. I could hear the sirens of dozens of police cars screaming up I-83 toward Mondawmin Mall. I paused for two seconds, caught my breath, silenced the voice of doubt (at least for a moment) and began.

"Saturday, we saw the best of Baltimore. We saw protests that were peaceful," I began. It was true. The preceding Saturday was April 25. A protest march of several thousand people had gathered at Gilmore Homes in West Baltimore and marched to City Hall to protest the death of Freddie Gray. It is hard to imagine; the march felt more like a celebration of life, a celebration of a voice that had long been waiting to be heard. It was an exhalation of frustration. I continued. "A small group of agitators turned that protest violent, and you saw remarkable restraint from our officers. Remarkable restraint."

What came next were words that we had fought long and hard to avoid having to say. When Police Commissioner Anthony Batts had been appointed at the end of 2012, he came to the city with a mission to modernize and reform the BPD. His ideas were forward-thinking, community-oriented, and had run afoul with many of the rank and file, who liked things the way they were, thank you very much. After a group of outside experts conducted an exhaustive and thorough review of the organization, we had developed a nearly 200-page strategic plan to move the agency forward. It had been a difficult two-and-a-half years as we had worked to root out corruption, hold officers accountable, celebrate those officers who were doing the right thing, and reconnect with a community that was as distrustful of the department as any community could be.

"This afternoon, a group of outrageous criminals attacked our officers. Right now, we have seven officers that have serious injuries, including broken bones, and one officer who is unconscious. We will do whatever is appropriate to protect the safety of our police officers and the people who live and work in the Mondawmin area." My voice was shaking with anger and disgust. I had spent the last forty minutes or so watching police officers wearing the same uniform I was wearing, the same

6

badge I had pinned to my chest, assaulted with bricks, chunks of concrete, and rocks the size of a fist. I had listened in horror and helplessness as officer after officer got on the radio begging for help. The sounds and screams that I heard on the radio will forever be etched in my memory. The sense that I had not done enough in the preceding days to stop this from happening will forever weigh on my soul. The shame—that my department had as much to do with the creation of this situation as those who were throwing the rocks—was a dark, hidden truth buried in the depths of my being.

I was conflicted about the situation we were in.

I did not believe my department had credibility with the people of Baltimore. Decade after decade of scandal and corruption had seen to that. Literally dozens of officers arrested for everything from assault to robbery to drug dealing to murder had weakened our standing. Video after video of officers assaulting people, cursing at them, were a daily staple of tweets and Facebook posts sent to us. We were still recovering from the impact of 2005, when we had made more than 100,000 arrests in a city of 630,000 people. And because of policies and laws, our internal affairs process, as good as it was, was shrouded in secrecy. I also knew that hundreds of officers were hardworking, dedicated, committed, and believed in what they were doing. Nearly two hundred officers had died protecting the City of Baltimore. Every year officers were shot at, broke bones, and had horrific car accidents, all in an effort to protect people in one of the most violent cities in America. We were truly a paradox of corruption and honor, greed and selflessness, honor and deceit.

Standing in front of the microphones, I knew it would be foolish of us to ignore the systemic reasons that had brought us here in the first place. Watching police car after police car roar up

I-83, one half of my brain begged them to move faster to help my brothers and sisters in blue. The other half was resigned to the knowledge that this was in some ways our due; that years of neglect and half-hearted measures had led us to this point. And I thought of Tennyson's "Charge of the Light Brigade":

"Half a league, half a league,

Half a league onward,

All in the valley of Death

Rode the six hundred."

CHAPTER 2

How We Got Here

Let's start at the very beginning, A very good place to start...

—RODGERS & HAMMERSTEIN, "DO RE MI"

To understand the distrust that exists between minorities and law enforcement today in the United States, we have to go back to the very beginning. Policing evolved in two primary ways in America: Night watchmen in cities, looking out primarily for fires, and slave patrols in Southern slave states. The latter drew a direct nexus to a real, visceral mistrust of police today in many communities. The slave patrols were men commissioned with the power to arrest, detain, and transport escaped slaves; they made their livings helping an establishment that imprisoned people of free will and forced them into servitude. Many of the patrols were state-sponsored, comprised of militia members, themselves coming from state military institutions. Even the name survives today. The slave patrols of the pre-Civil War era were known by several nicknames, including patrols and patrollers. We see that same title today, just in a different order—*patrol officer.*

Generation after generation of slaves existed in an environment in which enforcers of the law existed to keep them in bondage. Those are learned, generational experiences that pass down from one family member to the next. To ignore that fact is to ignore our own history as a country and the foundation of law enforcement in the United States. It is a history well remembered and understood in the African American community today.

Sadly, as I have traveled across the country teaching law enforcement, I have learned it is *not* common knowledge among today's police officers. This gap in understanding is a critical component in the mistrust that exists. As a country, we are only four (in some cases five) generations removed from slavery. In fact, in our cultural heritage, slavery on this continent existed for a longer period than has elapsed since its eradication. Families share the stories of their heritage with pride. For African Americans, too many have a shared family history rooted in white-controlled slavery, enforced by the rule of law, enforced by men of law enforcement.

After slavery ended, during the period of Reconstruction, the patrols and their tactics of abuse and intimidation did not.[1] As more and more municipal police organizations were formed, many of the tactics that had been previously used found their way into daily existence, now used against free men of color. Organizations like the Ku Klux Klan, which used barbaric tactics including murder and beatings, flourished across the South in the years immediately following the Civil War. They targeted freedmen of color and white sympathizers. It was a reign of terror that led to the enactment of federal legislation in 1870 and 1871 to stop the group.

While the KKK may have been temporarily stymied, the ideology of white supremacy was rampant. Starting shortly after the demise of the first iteration of the KKK, Southern states began to enact a series of laws that enforced segregation. This

---

[1] Hadden, Sally E. *Slave Patrols: Law and Violence in Virginia and the Carolinas*. Harvard University Press, 2003.

segregation applied to every aspect of life, from housing and education to transportation and water fountains. Black people in the South were controlled through state legislatures in what became known as Jim Crow laws—the name itself a pejorative term used to mock black people.[2] By 1890, the entire South would be racially segregated. Federal laws passed in 1866, in combination with the Fourteenth and Fifteenth Amendments meant to enfranchise newly freed slaves, were focused on voting rights and citizenship, leaving the states free to act as they pleased with regard to segregation.

As with nearly every law passed by a state, enforcement fell to local and regional police and sheriffs, the men of law enforcement. One generation removed from slavery and slave patrols, commissioned law enforcement officers were ensuring that black Southerners were kept in their place. This was codified by the 1896 *Plessy v. Ferguson* ruling, which held "separate but equal" to be the law of the land.[3] It would not be until 1954, in the *Brown v. Board of Education* decision, that this would be overturned.[4] Again, here we must look at learned history, the family history passed from one generation to the next. Many African American families living today have relatives who were alive during the enforcement of Jim Crow laws by police officers. That shared history has a real impact on the next generation's view of law enforcement.

In 1915, the KKK rose again, and there are documented cases across the South of law enforcement officers belonging to the KKK. The very people entrusted with upholding the law were part of a radical organization with a deep-rooted history of hatred and violence toward Southern black people. By the 1920s,

---

[2] Nittle, Nadra Kareem. "Understanding Jim Crow Laws." ThoughtCo. Accessed January 27, 2018. https://www.thoughtco.com/what-is-the-definition-of-jim-crow-laws-2834618.

[3] Plessy v. Ferguson (1896).

[4] Brown v. Board of Education of Topeka (1954).

approximately 15 percent of the nation's white population had enrolled in the organization. On August 8, 1925, 40,000 members of the KKK marched down Pennsylvania Avenue in Washington, D.C., wearing the robes that had become a symbol of racial hatred and fear. Regrettably, law enforcement association with the KKK has not ended. As of February 2018, there is still public reporting on police officers who have connections to the KKK; the hatred is still alive and well, and disturbingly in some cases wearing a police uniform.

Throughout the period of Jim Crow, lynching (extrajudicial killing by mob, often but not always by hanging) was a method of systematically intimidating and terrorizing black Southerners. Lynching became so accepted that the act was often photographed to be turned into postcards. Parents would bring children to watch lynchings and then be photographed with the hanging body. More than 200 bills were submitted in Congress to make lynching a federal crime. Not one of them passed both chambers. Several states adopted anti-lynching laws with little to no enforcement. In most cases, law enforcement made no serious effort to stop or investigate these extrajudicial killings. Police officers stood by and did nothing. At worst, some participated. In the extremely rare instance of a prosecution, sympathetic all-white juries would not convict the defendants. African Americans were barred in many states from serving on juries and had no voice in the process. The Equal Justice Initiative reports 3,959 people were lynched between 1877 and 1950.[5] These lynchings took place for any reason, from alleged crimes to looking at someone the wrong way. According to the NAACP, 27.3 percent of the people who were lynched were white, most because of their support for African Americans in the United States.[6]

---

[5] "Lynching in America: Confronting the Legacy of Racial Terror." Equal Justice Initiative. Accessed August 29, 2018. https://eji.org/reports/lynching-in-america.

[6] "History of Lynchings." NAACP. Accessed September 10, 2018. https://www.naacp.org/history-of-lynchings/.

At the height of the Civil Rights movement, beginning in the late 1950s and into the 1960s, police officers were at the forefront of the attempt to stop African American citizens from achieving equal enfranchisement. The reports, the news stories, the pictures; are all well documented. Birmingham and Selma, Alabama are synonymous with the struggle for equal treatment. Images from that era of police unleashing fire hoses, dogs, and riot batons on unarmed black men, women, and children will forever be scarred in the American consciousness. These were the tactics of law enforcement across the South. We cannot and must not ignore the impact of their actions on the understanding of law enforcement today, especially in communities of color. These experiences were a formative part of childhood for most black baby boomers. Even if they were not directly affected, they saw people who looked and felt like them attacked by police officers. Those images are searing and not easily forgotten.

I will explore present issues in a bit. It would, however, be negligent of me not to say that these few short paragraphs will never capture the horror felt by so many people, and they cannot atone for the injustice that was inflicted upon so many. They will never make what happened right, nor should they. It is my hope that if we can start with a base of knowledge and common understanding, then we can begin to peel back the layers of mistrust and animosity that are so palpable in America today.

If my experience has taught me anything, it's that the largest disconnect between police and the communities they serve, especially communities of color, is a lack of basic understanding on both sides. While both sides lack knowledge, *the onus falls on police departments* both to learn and to explain. Police departments serve their communities. They are paid by their communities. They exist for the sole purpose of protecting their communities. It is only logical, then, that they be the ones to reach out to reach and learn from their communities.

I hear from police officers across the country, "They just don't get it; until you strap on a badge and a vest, you'll never understand." There is some merit to that statement. The role of policing is so nuanced, varied, and diverse that it takes years to fully understand the job. There is no forty-five-minute PowerPoint presentation that can adequately encapsulate what it is like to be a police officer and to make the decisions required, sometimes in a few short seconds.

That same thing is true, however, of the experiences of many millions of Americans. Their experiences at the hands of police officers cannot be simply understood through a recitation of the facts around the circumstances of their encounters. This is a hard concept for police officers to understand. Officers are fact-based, evidence-driven creatures. The very nature of the job requires you to sort through emotion and drama, to explore only the facts. Police reports are written using facts. Police officers testify using facts. Juries decide cases using facts. So, naturally, when assessing a police-citizen encounter, police officers will look at the facts of the situation, divorced from any emotional connection or context to the situation. Officers will then render a verdict of justified or not justified based on the facts of the encounter. And with justification comes a moral certainty: the officer did no wrong. They will say the officer acted within the scope of his or her training, so what's the problem? What did you expect them to do?

What is lost in this process is the ability to understand, at an emotional level, what the experience was like for the person involved in the police encounter. That experience is multiplied exponentially when we take into account the impact of social media. Failing to understand how someone felt, how their learned and shared knowledge impacted their understanding of the encounter, how their previous experiences with police became a part of this new encounter, feeds and deepens the divide. Both sides feel morally vindicated, just in their actions and response. Both sides blame the other, and the cycle continues. And with each iteration of the cycle, the damage to a police department's trust and legitimacy grows. In today's age of rapid information sharing through social media platforms, that damage extends to law enforcement agencies across the country.

We've seen the deadly impact of this cycle. The rise in ambush-style attacks against police officers is well documented.[7] Five police officers in Dallas were assassinated in 2016 because of the view one person had about police: a view that was doubtless affected by numerous incidents sparking outrage, and in cases that will be discussed later, biased national reporting on police use-of-force incidents. And as I write this, two police officers were killed, shot through a window, while they were eating lunch. A widely perceived lack of concern on the part of police departments is literally leading to the deaths of police officers. The community faces the same level of impact from this disconnect. Officers become more protective, more insular, and more aggressive in communities they serve, partly out of fear and partly out of anger.

The anger in many police departments is real and understandable. It is a cliché, but often the best clichés are true; the vast, overwhelming number of police officers in this country do their jobs every single day with pride and honor. They strive to serve their communities with integrity.

---

[7] "Ambush Killings of Police Officers Has Hit a 10-year High." *The Washington Post.* November 21, 2016. Accessed August 29, 2018. https://www.washingtonpost.com/news/wonk/wp/2016/11/21/ambush-killings-of-police-officers-has-hit-a-10-year-high/?utm_term=.1afeed9f5e6d.

This isn't just rhetoric. There are data and facts that back this up. In 2011, 62.9 million people had encounters with American police officers.[8] From calls for service to traffic stops to arrest reports, one in four people in the United States had an experience with a cop. That is a remarkable number when you consider there are about 800,000 police officers in the United States.[9] Move forward one year, look at Department of Justice statistics, and the numbers become even more compelling. In 2012, there were 12,196,959 arrests. In that same year, there were 410 uses of deadly force by police: .00003 percent of total arrest numbers. These represent an infinitesimally small percentage of police encounters. In other statistical analysis, it might be considered so small as to be an aberration. From a policing perspective, there isn't a national problem. The numbers justify it.

There are two issues with this justification. Firstly, the use-of-deadly-force number is self-reported, with no clear guidelines for reporting. This makes the numbers difficult to gather into a reasonable study. That is not to say the number is unreliable; it *does* mean the number cannot and should not be used as absolute proof. Anytime you rely on self-reporting with no guidelines, you leave open the possibility of data omission, either by error or choice. The second and far more serious issue with these numbers is the removal of the human experience.

Let me be as clear as possible, from my vantage point, at least. There will be times when a police officer must use force. There will be times when a police officer must shoot and injure or kill someone. That is a reality. There is no getting around it. Having said that, *every* time there is a deadly use of force, there is a real human cost associated with that use of force. A family has lost a loved one. Friends will mourn a loss. These are not arbitrary

---

[8] Langton, Durose. U.S. Department of Justice Office of Justice Programs Bureau of Justice Statistics rev 2016

[9] U.S. Department of Justice, Census of State and Local Law Enforcement Agencies, 2008

things. Human emotion is a driver that is as real and tangible as any other part of our decision-making process. And it isn't just friends and family who are affected. A community is affected as well. Those who trust and support police will find themselves in pitched arguments against those who do not. Those who do not trust police will automatically assume the worst based on their own experiences and perceptions.

That was our experience in Baltimore with any number of use-of-force situations, in-custody deaths, and police-involved shootings.

One in-custody death stemmed from an attempted arrest that turned into a fight. During the fight, the suspect suffered a massive heart attack and died. The medical examiner's conclusion was that a combination of cocaine and severe dehydration, coupled with the intensity of the fight, led to the heart attack. The exam was also clear that the only sign of physical injury was one baton strike to the leg, which was consistent with the officer's use-of-force report. The officers were later filmed performing CPR in an attempt to save the suspect's life. An extensive review by both the state's attorney's office and an independent group of outside experts determined there was no evidence that the officers had used inappropriate force. The family, however, remains convinced to this day that officers beat their loved one to death.

This is the situation faced by police departments across the country in New York, Minneapolis, Sacramento, Los Angeles, and Ferguson. Each use of force by police officers nationally becomes a steady drip of perception-fueling experience.

Yet, it is the facts and figures, the letter of the law, that police departments continue to use to justify encounters. Their reliance on facts, devoid of context, explanation, or understanding, does more damage than good. There is a better way. A human way. It just requires a willingness to change.

It would be easy to conclude at this point that I hate police officers. Nothing—*nothing*—could be further from the truth. I still bleed blue in my heart. I have the crest of my badge tattooed on my leg. I travel the country nearly every week working with police departments large and small. In my heart and soul, I believe law enforcement to be a noble calling.

Real courage and real leadership means developing the ability to assess the things you are doing right and to be open to correcting the things you are doing wrong. For far too long, police departments have been doing it wrong. While investigations have found some departments deliberately acting with malice, that is not the case with the vast majority of the 19,000 or so police departments in this country. Quite simply, police departments are resistant to change of any kind. There is a better way. It doesn't just require a willingness to change, it requires a demand for change, from both inside and out.

CHAPTER 3

Homicides Drive Policing

You can't get there from here!

—A MAN IN A GAS STATION OUTSIDE OF HENNIKER, NH

W hen I was eighteen years old, I took my first solo road trip. I'd never driven outside of Connecticut before. This felt like a very grownup thing I was doing. I was excited; this was a trip on par with the expeditions of Lewis and Clark or Sir Edmund Hillary!

There is something about the freedom of being in a car alone that lets the mind wander. I can't remember all the groundbreaking, revolutionary ideas that were coming to me. Knowing me, I'm quite certain that I came up with a way to solve world peace, eradicate hunger, and make a million dollars by the age of twenty-five. (Side note: none of those things happened.) That's always been me, though. I love to take big ideas and break them down into tiny pieces. It's almost a form of meditation. While I have no idea what epic problem I was dissecting, I do know I got lost. Very, very lost. I was driving to see my best friend from high school. He was going to New England College in Henniker, New Hampshire, and I was on my way there. While I have no actual proof to validate my belief, I am convinced people from New Hampshire only want tourists to visit the beach and perhaps some leaf-peeping in the fall, but that's it. I hold this belief because there are *no road signs* off the highway. None. Well, at least there weren't in 1996.

I was lost, and I was mad. I had my printed-out directions from the greatest invention of all time: MapQuest. Surely its precision guidance would lead me safely to my destination. That trust came to a crashing end as I realized I was hopelessly lost in the state of no road signs. Now, like most men, I firmly believe that no one is truly lost: you just haven't driven far enough in one direction. So that's just what I did until I started to run out of gas. Broken and defeated, comforted by the knowledge that surely Lewis and Clark must have asked for directions at least once, I stopped at a local gas station to fill up and…yes, to ask for directions.

Walking into the little cinderblock storefront, I found a man in overalls sitting on a three-legged stool. He looked as old as the building itself. For that matter, so did his overalls. Mustering all the humility I could, I asked him if he could tell me how to get to New England College. His weathered face scowled at me, and in a thick New Hampshire accent he said, "You can't get there from here."

What madness was this? Of course I could. *There were roads.* They connected to each other. I wasn't driving an oxen train across a frozen tundra. Surely my 1992 Acura two-door could make the trip!

Eventually, we worked it out. His statement, though, stuck with me. It was one of those life-defining moments. I didn't get it at the time.

I would in the years to come.

It wasn't that I couldn't "get there from here." It was that I had been doing the wrong thing in the first place. He took one look at me and knew I was an eighteen-year-old kid who had jumped in a car, never checked a map, didn't plan the right amount of fuel, didn't check my tires or oil, or anything else. And he was right. I wasn't doing the right things to get there in the first place.

It's one of those things that's stuck with me through life. Anytime I've been in a less than desirable situation, I ask myself, "Can I get there from here?" In other words, am I doing the right things to get where I need to be in the first place? I have not always managed to get where I wanted to get, because I wasn't doing the right things in the first place.

The interesting lesson that I've learned throughout my life is that I rarely find myself in a stupid place because of intentional wrongdoing. Often, it's because I was going with the flow. I was taking the easy path. I wasn't taking the time to challenge myself or to think critically through an issue. And so it was that in April 2015, the BPD found itself unable to get there from here.

I can state with absolute certainty that Baltimore is one of the most unique, beautiful, and amazing cities in the country. Surrounded by Philadelphia, New York, and Washington, D.C., it never had the chance to become a "famous" city. Yet it encapsulates the very best of all of them, without pretense, expense, or drama. We have major league sporting teams (including the greatest football team of all time), opera houses, amazing food, a gorgeous inner harbor, the National Aquarium, and a tapestry of neighborhoods rich in diversity and their own special culture.

It is also a city of unimaginable violence, desperation, poverty, and not-so-hidden systemic racism. It is a city awash with food deserts, lackluster public transportation, more potholes than are reasonable, and a culture of brutality that at times is shocking to behold. It is a city where, during my career, a family of six was murdered while they slept because of their cooperation with police; where a three-year-old girl was murdered in her grandmother's lap by a stray bullet; all without any public outrage. And yet I love this city with all my heart. It does that to you. Slowly, like a song that bores into your brain, you will fall in love with Baltimore.

There are any number of reasons that Baltimore is where it is today. Poor planning led to an economic base that at one time was almost entirely dependent on the steel industry. As those jobs dried up, people began to leave the city, making it harder to find work. At its height, Baltimore had a population of over one million people. Today, that number stands at just over 600,000. Like a lot of American cities, the influx of drugs in the 1970s and 80s resulted in a shocking rise in its crime and murder rate. Books and TV shows have been written about Baltimore's staggering homicide numbers.

For people who are trapped in poverty without the benefit of a truly functional educational system, there weren't (and still aren't) a lot of options. Crime, drugs, and drug dealers all became a normal part of survival: not life, *survival*. That isn't hyperbole. You can ask just about anyone who has been a cop in this city for any length of time, and they can tell you about working a homicide scene on one end of a block, body still on the ground, while kids play on the other end. Incidents that would be shocking in any number of places across the country are a part of daily existence for far too many in Baltimore.

The segregation and systemic racism in this city are real. If you look at a map of Baltimore and put an L right in the center of the city, you can see the disparity in black and white. The L that runs from North Baltimore through to Federal Hill and then across the southeastern part of the city comprises our universities, hospitals, high-dollar residences and apartments, entertainment, and some of the best restaurants in the world. Oh, and mostly white residents. Step outside of the L, and that's the Baltimore so accurately portrayed in the HBO series *The Wire*. You can literally see it on a map.

In my own police department, the segregation was real as well. Through 1966, African American officers were quarantined in rank, meaning that a black officer could never supervise a white officer. Many of the city's first African American officers were not permitted to ride in departmental vehicles. Instead, they had to take a public bus out to their foot post. Maryland was one of the many states where a black man could not legally marry a white woman until *Loving v. Virginia* was handed down.[10] But court decisions and new laws don't change old ideology. There are places in the city and the surrounding county where the Confederate flag is still flown with pride. Baltimore suffered its own version of white flight. As African Americans moved into a neighborhood, white people fled to the country.

Then began a nearly three-decade-long obsession with the homicide number. Everything the police department and a good chunk of city government focused on had to do with the homicide number. Every day was a constant battle to lower that number. It became an obsession with local media featuring story after story counting the number of homicides each day, with comparisons and charts that showed year-over-year and year-to-date progress or decline. There is a Catch-22 to all of this. Of course, the number is important. Each one of those numbers is a human life lost, a family devastated, and a neighborhood victimized once again. It only makes sense that it would be a priority for the police department and local media. However, over time it became the *only* metric that mattered.

This near-universal obsession with the number led to a lot of short-sighted decisions and reactions from both city leaders

---

[10] Loving v. Virginia (1967)

and the police department. Enforcement strategies were built singularly around reducing the number of homicides. Sure, burglaries and robberies were important, but only if solving them led to information about a murder. Or if they generated just enough public outrage to warrant media attention. Pull over a car for doing 65 mph in a school zone? You better make sure that the person driving that car is a bad guy with a gun; otherwise, you're just wasting your time. Day after day, year after year, police commissioner after police commissioner had one mission: drive down the homicide number at all costs.

The "at all costs" part is important. Really important. I can remember attending roll calls in the Eastern, Southeast, and Northeast Districts, where commanders of various ranks were emphatic: "Lock up every swinging dick." "No free passes today—everybody goes." "Clear those corners. I don't care how you do it—get it done." The message from up on high was clear. Do whatever it took to stem the tide of violence. Whatever. It. Took. I was a part of this process. It is one of the great regrets of my career. At the time, though, it seemed perfectly normal and appropriate.

I worked in a plain-clothes unit in the mid-2000s. We wore street clothes, drove unmarked vehicles, and the only things that identified us as police were the badges we wore around our necks, which most of the time were kept hidden. A vital component of our job was to be able to cruise through neighborhoods unnoticed, to catch crime as it was happening. Plain-clothes units were feared throughout the city. We didn't answer calls for service, we couldn't be distracted by fake 911 calls, and we could go where we wanted in our district when we wanted to. We adjusted our hours to match crime trends and tried to be unpredictable. That was the idea in theory, at least. In reality, there are only so many unmarked vehicles, and our little green and black Chevy Cavaliers were pretty easy to spot. In a lot of the neighborhoods where I worked, I stuck out like a sore thumb. At 6'1", with blond hair, blue eyes and (thanks to my Germanic ancestry) skin that might as well have been translucent, I was hard to miss. It didn't take long for people to spot me from blocks away. It wasn't our job to develop complex cases. We followed leads where they took us, and we executed a fair number of search-and-seizure warrants. More complicated cases, however, were left to the drug unit to investigate. Our job was to have an immediate impact on crime. There was an ethos in our tight-knit group; you had to produce. And producing meant making arrests.

It was a routine day for my three-person unit to go out and arrest ten to fifteen people a day. Every day. And it was easy. Spend ten minutes learning the Maryland Annotated Code, and you can find any number of ways to make an arrest. On a slow day, just add the *A* for attempted or *C* for conspiracy to any charge. A group of you are walking toward a drug dealer to make a purchase? That's conspiracy to purchase a controlled dangerous substance, no free passes today—everybody goes. None of this was done with malicious intent. If you had asked my twenty-five- or twenty-six-year-old self, I would have insisted we were making the city safer. Arrest the buyers, the dealers move. The dealers move, the violence drops. The violence drops, the homicide number goes down. Replicate this belief across an entire department, and you can see how in one year we made more than 100,000 arrests.

The danger in this approach is that, numerically, it *does* have an impact on crime. The numbers *do* go down. The homicides slow. The media coverage eases up, and commanders can take a little less Zantac or Pepto before going to CompStat (short for Compare Statistics)—the dreaded, often feared weekly crime meeting. Some of the people who are arrested have really good information. That information is used to develop bigger and bigger cases. Really bad guys with guns start getting picked off by federal prosecutors. Seemingly all is moving in the right direction. Even today, on Twitter, many will argue vociferously that this was (and still is) the right strategy to end violent crime. The supporters of this strategy, either through a lack of understanding or deliberate indifference, ignore two critical failures of this policy.

When your primary goal is the reduction of homicide through aggressive enforcement action, you need aggressive officers. You need people who are willing to work in the worst possible conditions, for extended hours, without fear. You need people willing to go into neighborhood after neighborhood and extract the worst of the worst offenders. In *Inclusive Police from the Inside Out*, Workman-Stark writes about the "us versus them" mentality that begins to take hold in police culture—the sense that "we" the police are the good guys and everyone else are the bad guys.[11] This phenomenon is not new; police culture began to be studied with regularity in the 1960s.

The question then becomes, what happens to a group of police officers who are exposed to the worst elements of society on a daily basis, told to do whatever it takes to reduce crime, and then are sent out (with very little supervision or training) to accomplish the mission? Well, in a lot of cases, incredibly good police work happens. Heroic officers emerge, facing the most dangerous and deadly situations to bring peace to an embattled neighborhood; detailed, meticulous investigations proceed into those bringing a plague of violence and destruction to streets and neighborhoods across Baltimore. These women and men are and will always remain true heroes in my eyes. They give everything of themselves for people they will never know.

---

[11] Workman-Stark, Angela L. *Inclusive Policing from the Inside Out*. Cham: Springer International Publishing, 2017.

However, a darker, more sinister type of officer can also emerge. And their behavior is as disturbing and twisted as it comes. They use the power of their office, the authority of their badges to bully, intimidate, abuse, and in some cases terrorize people. They do it in the name of justice, but their actions cross the line between aggressive policing and criminal behavior. In 2014, Mark Puente, writing for the *Baltimore Sun*, published a series of stories documenting some of the abusive and illegal behavior of BPD officers.[12] It was a shocking and alarming in-depth look at the very worst behavior of the BPD. His work won him the Columbia University Graduate School of Journalism's Paul Tobenkin Memorial Award for reporting on racial or religious hatred, intolerance, or discrimination in the United States and the Institute on Political Journalism's Clark Mollenhoff Award for Excellence in Investigative Reporting. For the community, the series was proof that years of complaints about abusive policing had been justified. For many of us on the inside, it was a shocking, appalling view of things we had often heard rumored but had never before seen. This was the relative in the room whom we all knew had a problem but hoped would go away.

I do not claim innocence in this process. I was as much a part of the arrest machine as anyone else. Anyone who worked on the street with me as an officer or sergeant will tell you I had little tolerance for illegality. I had a quick temper and was even faster with my cuffs. I was not afraid of a physical confrontation, and I knew the Annotated Code front to back. There are people walking the streets of Baltimore today with scars I gave them years ago in fights leading to arrests. I made some good arrests. I got people with illegal handguns off the streets, and drug dealers, and violent criminals. I also made a lot of what I see now as unnecessary arrests. I thought I was doing my job. I was wrong.

---

[12] Puente, Mark, and Algerina Perna. "Sun Investigates: Undue Force." *The Baltimore Sun.* Accessed August 30, 2018. http://data.baltimoresun.com/news/police-settlements/.

It is not easy to make that admission. I'm not saying that I broke laws. I was very clear about the moral line that should never be crossed. I am saying I used the authority given to me by the state in a way that, at times, did far more harm than good.

The arrests we make as police officers have long-term consequences. When those arrests are of the right people, for the right reasons, they can bring a neighborhood much-needed peace and safety. They can give validation and vindication to victims of crime. When they are used as an obligatory response to an increasing homicide number, they only perpetuate a cycle of mistrust and outright hatred of police. Everyone we arrested had families, friends, and coworkers who would judge our actions based on their perception of the person they knew, but I don't know that any of us were thinking that far in advance. We thought we had to get the homicide number down.

When you do this day after day, week after week, year after year, damage is done. The community comes to think of a police department as being at war with citizens, and frustration becomes palpable, expressed in word and deed. Those words only cement the belief in police culture that everyone is complicit. "They" are letting this happen to "their" neighborhood. "They" are choosing not to help, not to provide information. "They" could make it all stop if they wanted to. Why can't "they" see that we are just trying to do our jobs? And the cycle continues.

I lived it. I have distinct memories of arresting someone and a whole block of people emptying out of their houses to scream at us, throw bottles, and hurl unrepeatable epithets. I remember thinking, how can they hate us? Don't they see what this guy is doing? Don't they know how bad he is? Cloaked in an armor of moral certainty, it is easy to disregard complaints and concern as unwarranted protest in our holy quest. It would be years before

I started really working with community groups and I could see the impact; I started to hear stories of cops gone wrong, or good cops who treated everyone with contempt. The process of seeing with new eyes was not an easy one. It meant that I had to question everything I had done and everything I had been taught.

This is why I talk about systemic issues. There are lots of examples of bad cops in the BPD—reams of stories, and countless hours of video. But when you compare them with the thousands and thousands of officers who served with pride and dignity, something doesn't add up. The sum doesn't equal the equation. It is only when you start to look at the system as a whole that you see the issues, bright as any neon sign.

The system itself is designed to do one thing: arrest people. If you think about it, it's a zero-sum game. There aren't a lot of tools police officers have at their disposal to solve an issue. They can mediate the dispute or make an arrest. That's it. So, when an officer is on scene, aware that other calls are waiting to be answered, they have to make quick, timely decisions about how to resolve a situation. When not legally required to make an arrest, the tactic most often used is separating two parties with an obligatory warning: "If I come back here, everyone is getting arrested." Maybe there is an exchange of information between two parties, or a report is taken. Then it's off to the next call.

If we want to change the way communities and police interact, it is not enough to simply give officers more training. We also have to change the system they operate in. We have to change the very operating basis that guides how police do their jobs, and we have to change the expectations a community has for their police department. If we don't change the system itself, any training for the individual officer is wasted. It is lost in a systemic process that will overwhelm any individual. That's not to say that training isn't important. It is. After all, the system is made up of individuals. Collectively, though, if we don't change the whole system, history will repeat itself. I can train all the kids in the world not to eat candy. I can show them the dangers and work to convince them that vegetables are a better option. But if they walk out of that training into a room full of candy, it's only a matter of time.

I'll talk more about the system itself later. For now, it is important to understand the way the BPD was operating for years. Our daily existence, over time, fed into a process of mistrust and abuse.

CHAPTER 4

A New Police Commissioner, A New Day

Treat the cause, not the symptom.

—Every doctor, everywhere

I t was Saturday morning, October 13, 2012, and I was sitting in the back of the BPD's mobile command vehicle at the finish line of the Baltimore Running Festival. A grueling marathon that serves as a prequalifier for the Boston Marathon, it snakes its way through almost the entirety of the city. I was the sergeant in charge of special events, which meant I was responsible for the security preplan and the implementation of that plan for the marathon. My team and I were reviewing our deployment when the side door of the command vehicle opened and in walked Anthony Batts, D.P.A., the newly selected police commissioner. I had only seen one photo of him previously, but he was instantly recognizable. We all scrambled to our feet in the tight rear compartment and in unison said, "Good morning, Sir." He came forward to me, extended his right hand, and said, "Hi, I'm Tony. What's your name?"

"Sgt. Kowalczyk," came the reply, without thought. It was as instinctive as breathing.

"No, not that, your first name," he responded with a smile. With that, I knew we had a very different police commissioner, indeed.

Tony Batts had spent nearly thirty years as a police officer in California. Starting with the Long Beach Police Department, he rose through the ranks to become chief of police. He then went to Oakland to be the police chief there. While in California, he had built a reputation as a problem-solving, community-oriented chief. In Long Beach, he created first-of-their-kind advisory boards to work with the community and bridge the gap between a distrustful public and the police department. He had a similar track record in Oakland, leaving after a new mayor was elected. It was that vision that had led to his selection as Baltimore's thirty-eighth police commissioner.

I had no idea at that moment that I was meeting a man who would open my eyes in a way that I had never dreamed possible, that he would become one of the greatest mentors a man could ever hope to have, and that he would drive me crazy nearly every day that I served as his director of communications. But that was a way off.

Shortly after the marathon, I took advantage of the opportunity to move to the media relations section, then called Public Affairs. I had daily interaction with the new police commissioner, or PC as we called him, but I didn't really have a good sense of who he was as a person. He played his cards very close to the chest. That all changed the last week of December 2012.

On Christmas Eve, a man named Kenni Shaw was walking to a corner store in East Baltimore. He was taunted by a group of men who berated him with comments about his sexual orientation. Their vitriol turned violent, and they started to beat and kick Mr. Shaw. His injuries were so severe that he had to be hospitalized. The image of his face, swollen beyond recognition, went viral in the city and prompted outrage among citizens and advocacy groups. Mr. Shaw's attackers were arrested, and on Saturday, January 5, 2013, dozens of residents and advocacy group members joined together for a march down the same streets where Kenni had been beaten. I was sent to pick up Mr. Shaw, who had just been released from the hospital, and escort him to the march. There we were joined by the police commissioner, who led the march through the streets in a sign of solidarity. It was at the end of the march that everything changed for me. The PC gave an impassioned speech about the need to treat all humans with dignity. And for the first time in my career, I watched the Police Commissioner of my department speak publicly about the need to treat people in the LGBT community as equal partners in a way that didn't feel like lip service.

After the group broke up, I was summoned over to the PC's car, and he asked, "How did I do?" I went to answer him and found that I couldn't talk. I wanted to say something, anything, but the words wouldn't come. Overcome with emotion, I looked him in the eyes as tears streamed down my face. I nodded at him, saluted him as per regulation, turned, and walked away. I was ashamed of my public display of emotion, but even more moved by what he had said.

When I was hired in August of 2002, I made the decision that I was going to be open about my sexual orientation. If people didn't like it, well, screw 'em. I was tired of hiding who I was. I knew I could do this job the same as anyone else. I'd gone through the same assessments, the same background check, the same psychological testing. I had as much right to be there as anyone else. In this alpha-male dominated profession, the idea of being judged for my sexual orientation was a powerful fear. My second week in the academy, on the advice of an academy instructor, I stood in front of my class of fifty fellow trainees and told them I was gay. It was incredibly difficult to do. But I wasn't going to hide who I was.

At the time in Maryland, I could have been fired for that admission. Maryland was one of many states that had no existing prohibition against firing a person based on their sexual orientation. I knew that by making the admission I was taking a huge risk, not just with the trust of my class, but with the very future I so badly wanted. As I write this in 2018, only twenty states have protections for LGBT employees. In the majority of this country, you can still be fired because of who you are, not what you do.

I never saw myself as a trailblazer, and I scoff at the idea now. As I moved up through the ranks, it wasn't always easy, and it wasn't always difficult. I was one of the first gay men in the department to be open about who he was. I was the first openly gay man to serve as a commander in the organization. I had people call me "faggot" to my face, refuse to back me up, torment me in public with innuendo and graphic displays meant to embarrass me. I was called on the radio once and asked to come to a scene of a domestic violence situation involving two women because they needed a "gay-to-English" translator. A lot of it bothered me; some of it was dangerous. And yet, the intolerance was the best thing that could have happened in my career. It motivated me to push myself harder than anyone else. I was the second person from my academy class promoted to sergeant and the first promoted to lieutenant and captain. I was determined to show the world that an openly gay man could do the job.

This isn't the case for everyone. Throughout my career, other officers would privately tell me how terrified they were to come out. They were afraid of the reprisal, the judgment, the blatant intolerance. They were afraid of losing the friends they had spent a career cultivating. My heart breaks for each of them; it is a horrible thing to have to hide who you are. It cuts to the bone when someone uses a discriminatory slur and everyone in the room laughs while you sit there in silence, the laughter only confirming that you need to hide your truth.

For all those challenging moments, I served with incredible officers—people who didn't care who I was, only that I could do the job. There were people who guided me, supported me, and helped me through some of the most difficult moments of my career. They stood as a bulwark against hatred and indifference. They showed me that there were good people willing to take a moral stand, and I wanted to be like them. They are incredible people and the very best of the Baltimore Police Department. There is no way to appropriately thank them all. They remain a part of my life to this day, and I am a better man because of them.

When I heard the PC speak that afternoon, I knew in an instant he was one of those people. Over the course of the next two years, I would get to know Commissioner Batts in a way few others would. In dealing with the myriad of issues we had to face, I saw a man whose singular focus was doing the right thing at the right time for the right reasons. He wanted to take care of the officers under his command, build stronger relationships with the community, and work to overcome years of racism, economic stagnation, and crime, which were strangling neighborhoods and residents and robbing them of a brighter future.

I never served in the military. I have talked to enough people who have, and the universal sentiment is that you get to see the true measure of a person when everything is at its worst. When you are in the foxhole with people, you will see what they are made of. Through every kind of imaginable issue, I stood by the side of Commissioner Batts and watched how he absorbed each hit against the department like a body blow to his soul. Then, he would dust himself off and say, "OK, we'll fix it. We'll get in front of it. Let us do what's right." Media portrayals and internal gossip never really saw this side of him. When you come in to reform any organization, the structure will resist change. The organization will resist the agent of change. That's human nature, and it happened during his tenure as police commissioner.

It wasn't all roses. We battled about issues all the time. I was probably as much a thorn in his side as I was an asset at times. I learned something about leadership in those moments, from the absolute willingness he had to listen to me even when he vehemently disagreed with me. Sometimes I won, sometimes I lost, but I always felt like I had a voice. Too many police leaders build a circle of acquiescent agreement around themselves. There is no one to tell the emperor he has no clothes. That was not our relationship.

Through many late night sessions, which I liked to refer to as our "time to hold Eric hostage sessions," we talked about discrimination, racism, bigotry, economic imprisonment, poor nutrition, poor sanitation, and the role all of that played in crime. In the first such session, as I was getting ready to leave for the day, the PC asked me who I thought had changed history the most. It was a loaded question, and I knew it. He was baiting me; this was more about my world philosophy and the way I thought than it was my view on history. Yet, like a lemming toward the edge of a cliff, I answered, "Henry VIII." It was not the answer he expected. I then spent the next forty-five minutes explaining my answer. Henry VIII's reformation led to a massive power redistribution in Europe, the diminishment of the influence of the Catholic Church, the expansion of

Lutheranism, which led to more and more people learning to read, which led to a more educated populace, which in turn led to scientific advancement. I talked about how his marriages would lead to a series of monarchs cumulating in the first Elizabethan era and the race against Spain to conquer the world. I could have picked any number of people from across the globe, but I wanted to rise to the test with an unexpected answer. I wanted him to see that I could take multiple tangents of history and link them together. I understood in that moment that he was evaluating how I thought about things. While I might be right or wrong in my assessment (I change my mind *all the time*), the important thing was that first session led to countless others in which we focused on Baltimore.

I learned how despair could cripple a community and how he wanted to shift the focus to repairing the health of neighborhoods to fix the underlying, root causes of crime. That the circular methods we had been using were as outdated as the Model T. By merely going after the crime, we were never addressing the *reason* that crime existed in the first place. Simply arresting bad people left a vacuum that others would step into. Take guns off the streets, more will pour in. Grab the drugs and more will find their way into the city. Tackle the reasons people are shooting each other in the first place, and you can start to make a lasting dent. It was a revolutionary approach to fighting crime in Baltimore and the country.

We had a lot of work to do.

CHAPTER 5

Exposing the Truth

*Those who cannot remember the past are
condemned to repeat it.*

—GEORGE SANTAYANA

The Police Commissioner's Board Room is on the fifth floor
of the Annex building, near the commissioner's office. At
first glance, it is an impressive room. There is a large, oblong
conference table with room for about twenty that dominates the
center of the room. Across the room is a wide bank of windows
with views out onto President Street, the fallen police memorial,
and Shot Tower, which at the time of its construction was the
tallest building on the east coast until the completion of the
Washington Monument in D.C. Around the walls are various
paintings of historic moments in Baltimore, including the defense
of Fort McHenry during the War of 1812. In September of 1814,
British naval forces, advancing on Baltimore, were stopped in
their tracks by valiant soldiers at Fort McHenry. Every time I
walked into the room, I would stop and look at the painting, even
if just for a moment. It was a powerful reminder of the good that
a few courageous individuals could do. The monument built to
celebrate their victory would later become the emblem for the
City of Baltimore, and it adorns the badge of every Baltimore
police officer.

I love history. Probably in an unhealthy way. I've made my peace with it. When I'm asked what my favorite history to study is, I usually just reply, "Yes." I mean, it is *all* fascinating. All of it. I don't understand how anyone wouldn't want to know how the town they live in came to exist. What did it look like in the days of yore? Like I said, I probably have an unhealthy level of interest. I'm the guy who stops to read all those signs on roads telling you that in 1775, this person ate mutton at this location for ten minutes. It probably takes me longer to read the sign than it took him to eat the mutton, but there I am, standing and reading. Jeff has long known this about me. He accepted with incredible grace that on our honeymoon in New Orleans, I was going to spend a day at the World War II museum. *Who would pass up that opportunity?*

It was with recent history in mind that I found myself in the Police Commissioner's Board Room on the morning of April 13, 2015. The Command Staff had just gone through an update on the previous day's arrest of Freddie Gray, and it was already clear there were issues. There was a problem with the taped statement that had been given to the initial investing team. It looked as if policies might not have been followed. And we had no idea how Mr. Gray had been injured. It was going to be an in-depth investigation. We were only a few months removed from the officer-involved shooting death of Michael Brown and days of subsequent community unrest in Ferguson, Missouri, and I was deeply concerned that we would be next. This case had all the required elements. As I was listening to the briefing, my mind kept flashing to the lessons learned from Ferguson. Be transparent, be up-front, don't defend, tell the truth no matter the political cost.

At the end of the briefing, I argued that we should ask the FBI to come in and investigate this case. Considering the real possibility that this would become a national story and given the severe credibility issues we had with the people of Baltimore, I did not think that we would be trusted or believed if we investigated the case on our own. I felt that asking the FBI to conduct the investigation would boost our credibility and give us some breathing room. I was making a tactical decision about a very human matter. That was my job: assess, consider, recommend a course of action. My role was unique. It was to do that assessment and consideration with media and public perception at the forefront of my mind. I understood the internal risks of bringing in an outside agency to investigate; it would send the message that we did not have faith in our own investigators. It would create a precedent that all future cases would need to be investigated the same way (not a bad idea). Finally, it would take all decision-making out of our hands. I was aware of all of that, and I didn't give a damn. We had had outside reviews after an investigation in the past. This was just building on what we had already done. It was a passionate argument on my part and was as close to being insubordinate as I had ever come in my career.

I've been accused of being arrogant for as long as I can remember. My Mom loves to tell the story of a time when I was an eight-year-old boy: I love astronomy *almost* as much as I love history. We had just learned in school that Pluto (it was still a planet then) was in a rare part of its orbit where it was closer to Earth's orbit than Neptune was. I just thought that was about the coolest thing ever. I was eight. It was a *big* deal. When I got home, I was excited to share my newfound knowledge and, much to my horror, no one believed me. I was so determined to prove that I was correct, I used the phone book to find the number for the local science center and called them. I put them on the phone with my mother so she could see I was right.

That has been me my whole life. I don't think I'm an arrogant person. My faith tells me to be humble. When I know that I'm right about something, however, I can be as stubborn and doggedly determined as any human you have ever met.

In this case, I knew I was right. I knew investigating Freddie Gray's arrest—and given the information that we had from the medical team, his likely death—on our own would be a huge mistake. The legitimacy of the investigation would be questioned, which would in turn leave lingering doubts in the mind of the public. There would be no independent verification of our work. which in the post-Ferguson environment would be seen as a cover-up. We would literally be giving a lit match to people who had fuel to burn us to the ground.

I also believe in the chain of command and respecting the decisions of the people above you. I made my argument, and I lost. I'm often asked if there are any decisions I regret during the Freddie Gray riots. The answer is always the same. Yes. This was it. If I could relive one moment of my life, it would have been to argue more forcefully, not to submit to the other senior commanders in the room. I had walked up to the line of direct insubordination and stopped. I should have gone further.

There is no way that I can prove that bringing in the FBI would have made a difference in the following days, or that they would have even accepted the case. I can, however, state unequivocally that in every interview I did, the legitimacy of our investigation was questioned. How do you convince an untrusting audience and an untrusting community that you have the standing to investigate your own? After so many scandals, so many arrests of police officers, so many news stories, in what possible way can you validate the credibility of your investigative team? I knew the people who were doing the investigation. They were good, solid people. Their hearts were in the right place, and they wanted to know what had happened as desperately as the rest of us. But my personal feelings about them were not the proof that Baltimore needed.

With the blessing of the police commissioner, I decided to do something truly unheard of. I reached out to Justin George, a reporter at the Baltimore Sun.

Justin is a tough, fair-minded, no-nonsense kind of guy. He was always up-front with me, and his stories were always fair. I didn't like a lot of them. In fact, of all the stories he ever wrote about the police department, there is only one that I truly liked. It was a moving, inside look at a grieving family. It was that story and my experience with him that led me to believe he would be the perfect person to embed in the investigation. I was thinking about the long-term picture and wanted a neutral, third party to be able to say that we had truly done everything in our power to properly investigate what happened.

Bringing Justin in was a very cloak-and-dagger operation. I called him and told him I needed to meet with him and wouldn't tell him why. He came down to headquarters and as surreptitiously as possible, he was escorted into my office. My office was my inner sanctum. Filled with personal mementos of my career, it had amassed an unusual collection. I have an inner five-year-old that I barely keep restrained at times. Minions kept my inner child very amused. Yes, the Minions from *Despicable Me*. Who doesn't love the Minions? People with no sense of humor, if you ask me. It started off as a joke; someone gave me a Minion toy. Which turned into two Minion toys. You see where this is going. In a very short time, my office was filled with them. I really feel like laughter keeps you sane, and Minions make me laugh.

Justin must have known something was up just from the fact that we were meeting in my office. I could count on one hand the number of reporters I had let into my office. This was my space, and it was sacred. I also believe that overhead fluorescent lighting is a cruel torture inflicted on those who must work inside. Its incessant buzzing and bizarre, diffuse light is enough to make me crazy. There, in my dimly-lit, Minion-infested office, I laid out my plan. Justin, if he agreed, would be embedded in the investigation, tied at the hip with the team. He would have access to everything, every interview, every piece of evidence; everything the team was doing, he could see and take notes on. There were two caveats to this embed: he was embargoed from telling anyone anything about what he was seeing; not his editor, not his friends. He could tell no one. The second part of the embargo was that he couldn't print or share a word of what he had seen until after the state's attorney's office made a prosecutorial decision. We didn't want him unduly influencing any part of the criminal justice process. Rather, this story was to be an after-the-fact look at everything we were doing. Again, I was focused on the long-term credibility of the organization.

He jumped at the chance.

I took a lot of flak about that decision internally. Investigations are the most closed and sacrosanct thing that a police department does. They involve gathering sources, and evidence, and interviews, and statements, and videos, and a million other things to get to the truth of what happened in a situation. To expose all of that, not just to an outsider, but to a reporter, was unimaginable. Yet my faith and confidence in Justin were unfaltering. I knew he would be fair in his reporting.

There was also a lot of consternation in the local media about the decision. I totally understood why. By picking one reporter, from one outlet, I was giving him an exclusive that anyone in that media market would have wanted. I empathized with their frustration as well. Over the course of two years, my team worked really hard to make sure we equally rotated our story pitches with all of the media outlets. No TV station wants to see another station get an exclusive story that they don't have. It wasn't an easy thing to do all the time; I actually kept a rotation log just to make sure we were cycling through everyone. It wasn't that there weren't great television and radio journalists in Baltimore. In fact, I'd put our reporters up against most of the national outlets. I just didn't think the story could be adequately told in a two-and-a-half minute story package.

Ultimately, it was the best decision I made. A few days later Justin would be tied at the hip with the investigative team.

A lot of decisions in those first few days challenged the status quo. We answered every question submitted, from anyone, anytime, anywhere. I was fearful of any news organization running the dreaded "declined to comment," or "did not return our calls and emails" line. That would only further the narrative that we were hiding information from the public. So, we set out to be as open and as transparent as we had ever been. There was tremendous pushback from our own department and the state's attorney's office. No one was used to releasing the volume and type of information we were so freely disclosing. To be clear, I did not have authority on my own to release any information. Every piece of information that was made publicly available— every single piece—went through a review process.

There were legitimate internal concerns about the information we were disclosing. Detectives worried about compromising witnesses, making source verification harder, or giving the wrong impression about something. The same was true with people in the state's attorney's office. They were concerned about compromising a jury and the possibility of impeachable witnesses. There were also irrational and self-serving concerns on both sides. I heard everything from "This will make us look bad" to "This is our call, not yours." Once again, I didn't care. I was willing to take all the heat necessary to ensure that the BPD's true story would be heard by all.

History had shown us how devastating the withholding of information was in Ferguson. It has shown us time and time again that when departments attempt to keep information from the public in a high-profile event, it only serves to galvanize those who believe your agency is corrupt. It is like pouring gasoline on a bonfire. I wasn't going to give them the gas.

There was a simple metric we used to evaluate each piece of information before it went out:

1. Will it help the investigation or hurt the investigation?

2. Will it help the department's mission or hurt the department's mission?

That was it. Every time I was told the investigation would be harmed, I dug deeper. "Tell me how. In what way? Use specifics. Don't speculate." It was a constant battle. It had to be. The default response of any detective investigating any crime is to hold onto every little bit of information because you never know what might break a case. The thing is, that is often a self-defeating ideology. In short order, on most cases, good detectives already have a sense of what they will and won't need. Everything else is icing on the cake. We didn't have the luxury of icing cakes this time.

The second question was a little trickier. It makes perfect sense that if something looks bad, nobody wants to put it out. We've seen that old game in politics, corporations, and policing. That shouldn't be the standard, though. And it wasn't for us. If the information we were going to put out was going to compromise public safety, or in some way prevent officers from doing their job, then we had a legitimate reason to withhold it. Otherwise, it went out. I didn't care if it made us look bad; we could deal with our reputation later. What we had to protect against was the growing concern that "the thin blue line" would protect itself. The only way to prevent that was either an outside agency doing the investigation or to be as transparent as possible. The adage "Sunshine is the best disinfectant" is true. We were going to let the sunshine in.

There was a lesson learned in all of this. The old way of doing things doesn't work anymore. We live in a world of twenty-four-hour news and rapid information exchange on social media. Someone will fill the void of information with innuendo and speculation. The majority of law enforcement agencies are still operating in the 1970s when it comes to disclosing facts about a case. They will release the information they want to release when they want to release it.

Far, far too often what you'll hear from a police department is, "We cannot comment on an open investigation." That is a load of garbage. There is *always* something you can say. You can talk about the process of the investigation, you can talk about the investigative team itself, you can talk about the investigative policies and procedures that are used in the investigation. There is *never* a reason for a police department not to provide some level of information about what's going on in a case. If the profession doesn't start to change the way information is provided to the public, nothing in the public's understanding will ever change. It's far too easy to say, "We can't get into that right now."

Who said this was supposed to be easy?

When the stakes are as high as they were in the situation we were facing, the responsibility to be as transparent as possible only increases. We knew that from day one, and Commissioner Batts saw it as well. He took a lot of hits for his willingness to be as open as we were. Had we chosen to operate under the old mentality, I can't imagine how much more devastating the consequences would have been. I'll talk about the outside reviews later, but I do want to make one point. All of the independent reviews commended the openness and transparency of the BPD.

CHAPTER 6

A City on the Brink of Disaster

If there is no struggle, there is no progress.

—FREDERICK DOUGLASS

I was never one to believe in love at first sight. It sounds like a Hallmark card run amok. Like a lot of couples in these modern times, Jeff and I met online. We talked online, through text messages, and then on the phone for a while before we met in person. There was something different about him. While I'd seen his photo and thought he was devastatingly attractive, it was his personality that pulled me in.

Our first date was sushi at a restaurant that I love. It was as much a test as a date. If you don't like sushi, we don't have a future together. I was not to be disappointed. I was dutifully standing on the appointed corner where we arranged to meet when I saw him for the first time. Here was this man I had been talking to walking toward me, a first-generation American whose mother and older sister were both born in Haiti. Somewhere in the back of my brain, I heard a voice say, "You're going to marry him." Clearly, that voice was drunk or oxygen-deprived. It was our first date. *Silence, you*! It would be months later that Jeff told me after our first date, he saved my address in his car GPS under the nickname "Hubs." Sometimes the stars align.

A native New Yorker, Jeff grew up in a Haitian American family in Brooklyn. He had joined the Army and to this day is still an active-duty soldier. We had a lot in common; that first date was unlike any other I had experienced in my thirty-odd years of life. We joke that we are still on our third date, and it's true. We were engaged six months later and married by the end of the year. Of all the decisions I have made in my life, going to sushi that night was the single best.

We had a lot of conversations about the role of policing while we were dating. His experiences in New York, along with those of his friends, had helped to form his vision of law enforcement. As a black man living in America, Jeff had his own experiences that were light years apart from my New England prep-school upbringing. Seeing the world through someone else's eyes can be a difficult thing to do. It means putting aside preconceived notions and being willing to learn. Listening to his experiences allowed me to learn about the African American experience in a powerful and moving way. I distinctly remember a conversation in which he relayed how excited he was when he turned twenty-five. For me, turning twenty-five meant that I got a discount on car rentals and car insurance. For him, getting to twenty-five meant he wasn't a statistic.

A shocking report from the NAACP detailed the following statistics:[13]

- In 2014, African Americans constituted 2.3 million, or 34 percent, of the total 6.8 million American correctional population.

- African Americans are incarcerated at more than five times the rate of whites.

---

[13] "Criminal Justice Fact Sheet." NAACP. Accessed August 30, 2018. http://www.naacp.org/criminal-justice-fact-sheet/.

- The imprisonment rate for African American women is twice that of white women.

- Nationwide, African American children represent 32 percent of children who are arrested,

- Forty-two percent of children who are detained, and 52 percent of children whose cases are judicially waived to criminal court, are African American.

- Though African Americans and Hispanics make up approximately 32 percent of the U.S. population, they comprised 56 percent of all incarcerated people in 2015.

- If African Americans and Hispanics were incarcerated at the same rates as whites, prison and jail populations would decline by almost 40 percent.

We can either conclude that African Americans—specifically African American men—are just predisposed to commit more crimes (which is an asinine nonstarter), or there is something fundamentally wrong with the criminal justice system. As a police officer, it is easy to apply anecdotal experiences to statistics and say that's a bunch of bunk. I've heard it before. I've also been told that you can make statistics say whatever you want, which to a degree is true. However, a simple Google search will show anyone how much research has been done on this topic. And the voluminous amount of research out there shows there is a clear problem in the criminal justice system. A report released in October 2015 by the United States Department of Justice showed dramatic sentencing differences in the federal system between white defendants and black defendants.[14]

This was the battle raging in my head the week of April 12–19, 2015. I was terrified that we were sliding down the same path that

[14] Rhodes, William, et al. "Federal Sentencing Disparity: 2005-2012." *Bureau of Justice Statistics (BJS)*, 2015, www.bjs.gov/index.cfm?ty=pbdetail&iid=5432.

we had seen a few months previously in New York following the grand jury return in the police-involved death of Eric Garner. I was even more concerned about becoming the next Ferguson. All the elements were there; a police department with a history of documented and perceived abuse, an unarmed black man clinging to life, and the arrival of protest groups from across the country. It was our job to explain to the world what was happening and to do everything we could to tamp down emotions.

My professional obligation was to do all I could to define for the world the circumstances surrounding the arrest of Freddie Gray and the subsequent investigation into his injury. It was an exhausting blur of a week that I do not fully remember. I know that we were answering media inquiries from across the country. We were doing everything that we could to push out as much information as possible. Our guiding purpose was transparency: define what happened, define the investigation, answer every question, every email, every phone call. Even now, it is hard to describe how intent my team and I were on making sure that we did everything we could to represent the hardworking men and women of the BPD to a global audience, with as much integrity and candor as we could.

On April 14, the Gray family released a photo of Freddie Gray in the hospital, and the world took notice.

I couldn't take my mind off the photo the family had released. It was emotionally devastating to see someone clinging to life, knowing that while the investigation would determine if the injury was intentional or a devastating accident, it had happened at the hands of your department. The face I saw in the photo was as much the face of Jeff as it was Freddie Gray. I was aware that under different circumstances, that could have been Jeff's face. This is no easier to write now than it was to experience at the time. On one hand, I had my professional obligation, which I was going to do with every ounce of my being, lest my city descend into chaos. On the other hand, I kept thinking, "Why? Why did this have to happen? Whatever the individual circumstances are, isn't this just another black man about to die because of police interaction? Not just police interaction, but my agency's interaction?" I'm aware that anyone reading this will think that I allowed my personal feelings to influence my thinking. I did.

Police officers are very good at compartmentalizing. You have to be, or you won't survive. There are only so many times you can see a dead body, tell a family that a loved one died, see the worst abuses that can be done to a child, before they start to impact your soul. You must find a way to make it all work or the job will tear you apart. This time I couldn't find a way to separate the two. Instead, it drove me. I wanted to make sure the world knew about the thousands of honorable police officers who came to work every day with noble intent. I wanted to make sure that everyone who was reading my words, hearing my voice, or seeing my face knew how invested the police commissioner was in reforming the department. The people of Baltimore needed to know the incredible strides the agency had taken toward alignment with their expectations.

On New Year's Day 2015, we held a news conference to talk about our reform efforts. Standing in a park in West Baltimore, surrounded by members of the community, the police commissioner talked about what one full year of reform had yielded. In that one year, 2014—the first full year of our reform efforts—we had reduced excessive force complaints by 45 percent, decreased discourtesy complaints by 54 percent, and cut police-involved shootings by two-thirds. At the same time, we had reduced crime in every major category to the lowest levels since the 1970s, save for our homicide rate, which was the second-lowest number since the 1970s. By every metric that you could measure, the BPD had hit a home run.

While policy and direction come from the top, it was the women and men who were out on the streets who had achieved these incredible results. I did not want their hard work to fall by the wayside. I could see how easily the media narrative was going to spin public opinion and how quickly that would destroy all the good work that had been done. That could not happen.

I was also motivated by the knowledge that this was the exact conversation the police commissioner had been having with me. Don't treat the symptom; treat the issue. Treating the symptom only creates space and opportunity for animosity to grow. I was under no illusion that now was the time to finally have that conversation. No one would have been listening; no one would have heard our cry. It was, however, proof of what he had been talking about. This horrific situation we were now in was the answer to all the critics in the department and in city government who said, "Stay in your lane," "You should only be talking about crime," "Who are you to talk about systemic, historic racism in this city," and "You're an outsider."

Well, here was the answer. A family about to lose a loved one, the world's media on the way, and a city on the brink of disaster.

CHAPTER 7

Eyes Wide Shut

Hey, hon, how are you?

—JAYNE MILLER, WBAL-TV 11 NEWS

H on" is to Baltimore as "Bless your heart!" is to the South. It is a universally understood call, greeting, expression of fondness, or "Hey, you!" Café Hon is one of the most notable attractions in the Hampden neighborhood of the city.

"How 'bout dem Os, hon!" is an expression of joy or sorrow, depending on how the Orioles are doing. It is as Baltimore as crabs and Old Bay, something everyone should experience at least once in their life. Hon has made its way to Broadway in *Hairspray* and is one of those things about Baltimore you come to love. It is one of the million little quirks that make Baltimore such an extraordinary place.

Every neighborhood in this city is distinct. Roland Park conjures images of parkland and multimillion-dollar estates. Federal Hill evokes a vision of Federal-style row homes, a magnificent city vista, and Cross Street Market, where every Friday and Saturday, you can find each of the city's universities represented with gusto. Fell's Point is one of Baltimore's oldest and most historic neighborhoods, right on the water, with pre-Revolution construction and cobblestone streets. Its where NBC's *Homicide: Life on the Street* was filmed.

I live in Mount Vernon, just north of downtown, which is an eclectic mix of every demographic you can think of, surrounded by French architecture and Gothic churches. It is home to the Washington Monument (the original one, not that Egyptian thing in D.C.) and the first-of-its-kind park that surrounds the monument.

I love walking through my neighborhood. Every day I find some new architectural detail I've never seen before. Every kind of food you can imagine is just a few short blocks from my front door. We have artists and hipsters, lawyers and musicians, upscale dining and great carry-outs. I've lived in this neighborhood longer than I have lived anywhere else on this planet. It grabbed hold of me and won't let go. I'm OK with that.

From the windows in my living room, I can see all the way to the edge of the city in Southwest, West, Northwest, and Northern police districts. It was in front of these windows that I found myself on the morning of April 19. I savored the silence of the early Sunday morning. Trees were beginning to bloom, and the bright green mixed with brilliant white of the dogwood trees flowering was a gorgeous contrast to Gothic church spires and dominant feature of the Fifth Regiment Armory.

My eyes locked onto the Armory and I thought of the days to come. I wondered with some degree of prescient foresight if the Maryland National Guard would be needed. I had just hung up the phone with Colonel Green from the Office of Internal Oversight, who had called to tell me that Freddie Gray had died. Everything would change now.

Jayne Miller is the lead investigative reporter for WBAL-TV 11 News in Baltimore. A no-nonsense, salt-of-the-earth reporter, her unmistakable voice was often a harbinger of my day becoming far more complicated. She has been reporting in the city for more than thirty years and can recount the details of everyone she had talked to throughout her career. She cares deeply about the city, and it shows in her reporting. In my role as director of media relations, two things about Jayne were clear right away; don't *ever* try to bluff her, and if she's calling she already has the story. In the early days of my tenure, the stories she already had were rarely good for the department.

My first real experience with Jayne as a reporter was watching her cover the department when I was a rookie. I couldn't understand who this horrible reporter was and why she hated the department. Of course, in those days, anyone who offered anything other than glowing praise was an idiot. Perception.

It would have been easy to write her off as an extremist police-hater. I heard a fair number of police officers say that she hated the BPD and would do anything to tear it down. Much like any family under attack, it was fine for us to criticize ourselves, but who was *she* to do it? And for the first few years of my career, I did just that. Ensconced in my moral certainty about the work I was doing, she became the extreme opposing voice. As I progressed through my career, I would start to see the merit of the story she was trying to tell—the alarm that she was trying to sound—of the warning that this would all turn around and bite us in the ass one day.

Jayne Miller has spent decades reporting on the abuses of the BPD. In her effort to give voice to the voiceless, she made a lot of enemies inside the department. I would learn as director that she also made a lot of friends. Officers who, frustrated with intractable obstruction, turned to her to try and right the wrongs that they saw. While I didn't agree with every story Jayne did, I learned to respect her and the story she was telling. When it came to the BPD, often that story was one of suffering and abuse at the hands of one of our officers.

Working with Jayne, it became clear that her mission wasn't to tear us down. It was to protect the city and to try to highlight how we needed to change. It wasn't just the BPD, either. Where Jayne saw injustice, corruption, or an attempt to tear down her beloved Baltimore, she would be there with a camera. Working with Jayne, it became clear that she didn't tell a story simply because she could; her drive came from being an eternal optimist. She sees the things that could be, that should be, and works to make them a reality. Not to like Jayne Miller's stories is not to like the ugly in the mirror of her reporting.

I was thinking about her that Sunday morning. I knew it was only a matter of time before my phone would ring and I would hear, "Hey, hon, how are you?" It wouldn't just be Jayne, of course; it would be the world. This was the moment that national and international media had been waiting for.

Forgive me if I sound callous, but that was the truth. This death would amp the story up a notch. They now had a new angle to report on. For days preceding the death of Freddie Gray, I'd been getting questions from the national networks about what we would do when he died. Not *if* he died, *when* he died. Would there be a news conference, where would it be, who would be there? They were planning their coverage, vying for the right angle to tell their story in a unique way.

The opposite was true of my local reporters. Horrified by the death of Freddie Gray, they attempted to tell the story in a responsible way. They weren't interested in ginning up drama or panic. Rather, theirs was some of the most honest, straightforward, and responsible reporting I have ever seen. Every week as I travel the country, I talk about my experience with local and national media coverage, and I give the same advice: "Treat your local media like gold. They were there before a crisis, they're with you during it, and they will be there long after the nationals leave."

There were some incredible national reporters and producers in the city. They did honest work with us and got the truth out to a global audience. However, what cannot and should not be ignored is the difference in the way the story was being relayed here in Baltimore versus what the rest of the world was seeing. It was our job to monitor the coverage, and there was a marked difference between the two. More on that later.

———•———

It is amazing in a moment of crisis how fast you can think, and how many things you think of. As we were preparing to announce to the world that Freddie Gray had died, I was thinking of how to get the message out responsibly, how we would have to urge peace, what the PC's remarks should look like, what would happen to my beloved city, what would happen to the officers on the street, could I work the words just enough to keep them safe, and what would Jayne say.

You might think it strange that in the midst of everything, I was thinking about one reporter, but it's true. I knew her voice would cut through and rise above all the others, and how she told the story would determine how a large number of the people of Baltimore would receive the news. They had been watching her for decades, and her voice mattered. If only we had been paying attention sooner.

Jayne's reporting on the corruption and abuses of the BPD stretched back further than my career. She didn't do gotcha journalism. Her focus was never fifteen-second shaky cell phone video that might have shown something out of context. Rather, her focus was on the same systemic issues of corruption, racism, poverty, lack of quality education, and desolate neighborhoods that we would come to focus on under Commissioner Batts. Her stories were an unyielding arc of coverage that should have been a warning to us all: We needed to do better. In the trenches of day-to-day work, it's easy to miss the big picture; she never did.

In order for good criticism and critique to be effective, one of two things has to be true: you have to be open to hearing it, or someone has to force you. For a very long time, the BPD had not been open to hearing the critique, and no one was really forcing us to listen. Rather, the response each time was to delve into the specifics of each situation Jayne was reporting. "Well, this was a unique situation…this officer didn't follow policy, but…our investigation is ongoing…in this particular case…" and so on. In those cases where the facts really did show that we didn't do anything wrong, that was an important component to get out. What we were missing, though, was the totality of the circumstances. Yes, you can parse each situation and pick them apart. Yes, you can use law and policy to justify actions. But that doesn't address the overall issue. If issues keep happening, if stories keep coming, that is indicative of a larger, systemic failure. And we just weren't paying attention. After all, the only thing that really mattered was getting the homicide number down.

Jayne wasn't the only reporter doing these stories. I already talked about Mark Puente's work. What is notable, and what makes Jayne's reporting different, is the length of time she had been doing it and the consistency of departmental abuse and failure that her reporting showed. Hindsight is 20/20, or so they say, and it is easy to go back now and connect the dots.

I'm forced to wonder, if we had started connecting the dots sooner, how events might have played out differently. Some former colleagues reading this will likely be enraged by what I'm saying here, and I understand their anger. This isn't about the thousands of officers who served with nobility; this is about the *system they were operating in*. And the evidence shows, the system wasn't paying attention. Jayne was.

CHAPTER 8

This is Our Ferguson

Great things are not accomplished by those who yield to trends and fads and popular opinion.

—JACK KEROUAC

I t is possible that I am the least trendy person alive. I have no idea who is popular, what music is topping the charts, or what I should be wearing. I tend to find a shirt I like and buy it in every shade of blue. There, shopping done. I'll go see new movies, and I try to keep my iTunes library relatively updated; I just would rather watch the news, read a book, or go to a great restaurant than worry about who's up and who's down. I could not care less about the Kardashians. I'm sure they're a very nice family. I just don't quite understand the obsession. I'm far more interested in learning about the impact of some cosmological event that occurred 1.2 billion years ago. It is what it is.

Policing, on the other hand, for all its tradition, is *very* interested in trends. Articles and conference headlines proclaim, with gusto, "The Top Five New Trends in Policing." This is not new. Coming out of the 1960s, think tanks, universities, and professional organizations did real work to modernize policing. Systems, organizational charts, policies, and procedures were examined with rigor. A lot of what was taking place was influenced, and rightly so, by events of the day. And thus began the last forty years of ten-year trends in law enforcement. You can look back decade by decade and see the solution to all things crime-related.

Early in the 1970s, the Police Foundation published one of the first comprehensive reports on professionalizing modern policing. The study, *Team Policing: Seven Case Studies*, was an in-depth look at a new way to fight crime.[15] It was a revolutionary approach to policing, challenging how things had been done since the 1920s. That led to a series of other studies in the 1970s and a movement to create more professional, intelligence-based policing. Metrics were established to measure the efficacy of law enforcement. Standards for training were more rigorously applied. The role of minority and female officers was more closely examined.

The influx of cheap narcotics in the 1970s led to a massive effort to combat them in the 1970s and exploded into the 1980s. In the early part of the 1970s, the Nixon administration declared "war on drugs," leading to the creation of the Drug Enforcement Agency (DEA) and the passage of the Comprehensive Drug Abuse Prevention and Control Act of 1970. This law would take a mishmash of laws originating from 1914 forward and organize them for the first time, including grouping drugs into specific categories used for enforcement and sentencing.

As drug crimes escalated into the 1980s, more and more agencies turned to aggressive enforcement tactics as a means of combating the drugs and violence. The era of mass incarcerations took hold. Lacking any comprehensive intervention and treatment efforts, more and more people were incarcerated for drug crimes. As of 2013, the United States had the highest incarceration rate of any nation in the world.[16]

---

[15] Sherman, Lawrence W., Catherine H. Milton, and Thomas V. Kelly. *Team Policing: Seven Case Studies*. Washington, D.C.: Police Foundation, 1973.

[16] "Bureau of Justice Statistics Home Page." Bureau of Justice Statistics (BJS). Accessed September 10, 2018. https://www.bjs.gov/index.cfm?ty=kfdetail&iid=493.

The first application of Broken Windows Theory, or zero-tolerance policing, was seen in 1973, following the passage of the Safe and Clean Neighborhoods Act in New Jersey. In essence, the policy was based on the idea that if there was zero tolerance for all crime, and enforcement action for even the most minor violations, major crime would not occur. Following a decade of increasing crime and tremendous violence, New York City also adopted the policy to reduce crime. This led to a lot of the mass arrests which I talked about previously. Because NYPD was using the policy with effect, a surge of departments across the United States adopted the same policy. Their efforts were further bolstered by the passage of the Violent Crime Control and Law Enforcement Act of 1994, known colloquially in that era simply as the Crime Bill. "Hot spot" policing became a critical component of this approach. Focused on crime data, policymakers would increase enforcement activities in targeted zones to fight crime. In 2012, a study showed that all this effort had a modest impact on reducing crime.[17] It did, however, have a dramatic impact on police and community relations, leading to the post-Ferguson *President's Task Force Report on 21st Century Policing.*[18]

This is a very short and very broad history of the last forty years. There is good research available that more closely examines the impact of each of these trends, and why they are no longer used. Some departments set and lead the trends, some departments follow them, and some departments do nothing at all. There are police departments in the United States today that have no written policies and procedures. Its mind boggling, I know. The only consistency is the consistency to follow whatever is trending now.

---

[17] Braga, A. "The Effects of Hot Spots Policing on Crime." *The Annals of the American Academy of Political and Social Science* 578 (2012).

[18] *Final Report of the President's Task Force on 21st Century Policing.* Washington, D.C.: U.S. Department of Justice, Office of Community Oriented Policing Services, 2015.

None of the trends address the actual root cause of crime. They are all geared toward enforcement, interdiction, and incarceration. By failing to engage with the root issue of crime in the first place, police leaders are just looking for new ways to invent the wheel. What *can* be shown throughout this period is ever growing mistrust of law enforcement by the communities it is meant to serve. I talked previously about the NAACP's research on systemic racism: They and others have done tremendous work looking at the tangential cost of mass incarceration, how the system becomes both learned and cyclical. The Independent Committee on Reentry and Employment, an independent body established in the State of New York to look at this issue, conducted a study finding that 67.8 percent of all released prisoners will reenter the system within three years of release.[19]

In the days leading to the death of Freddie Gray, a common theme of those protesting was the abuse, real and perceived, that they, their families, friends, and community had suffered at the hands of police. Not just from the BPD: police across the country. Protestors had come to Baltimore from all over the country. The injury, and now death, of Freddie Gray had compelled them to come and express their visceral frustration. Names of other people who had died in police custody were on the signs they carried, including Anthony Anderson and Tyrone West—two other black men who had died in BPD custody before they could be charged. (In those two cases, two independent reviews would find no illegality on the part of officers in either case; we instituted recommendations for policy and operational changes as a result.)

Beginning in 2007, my department invested a lot of resources, time, and energy into trying to build bridges with the community.

---

[19] *The Independent Committee on Reentry and Employment, Report and Recommendations.* Report. April 25, 2006. https://www.reentry.net/ny/search/download.128868.

These efforts, while driven from a good place, were doomed from the start. You can't reach out to a community with one hand while you're choking it with the other. It is all well and good to go into a community and talk about how important partnerships are and how much the community is a vital component of police strategy. Those words fall on deaf ears when Facebook posts, cell phone videos, and story after story highlight misconduct and disrespect. These were genuine efforts to connect with the community; we met with some success as a result. But bridge building was separate and apart from ongoing enforcement efforts.

Beginning in 2012, we started the process on a different footing. Commissioner Batts created advisory boards for every demographic we could think of. At the end of 2014, we had an advisory board for the African American, Latino, LGBT, youth, business, academic, and faith communities. They met with the police commissioner on a bimonthly basis, helping to develop policy and training. We created a Youth Explorer Summer Camp, an advisory board for family members of murdered loved ones, and commissioned a strategic reform of the organization. These efforts constituted real movement toward changing the operating ethos of the BPD in how we fought crime and connected with our community. We just didn't have enough time.

As I walked out my door to drive to City Hall, I knew everything would be different. The tension in the city had been building for the past week.

It is hard to describe a city on edge. You could feel the unease in the air, almost as if you could touch it. You could see a look of worry on people's faces as they walked the streets. Hushed conversations in restaurants and heated rhetoric on television created a sensation that something was about to break; it was just that no one knew what it was going to look like.

Pulling into the cobblestone lot in front of City Hall, I was once again struck by the building's beauty. Construction started on the Second Empire-style building in 1867. With its soaring dome supported by columns, imposing front, and high roofline, it was exactly what a city hall should look like. Its magnificent exterior is betrayed by a strange mix of a 1980s interior interspersed with granite and marble. The City Council Chamber is beautifully ornate, while the meeting rooms look like they were pulled from some fictional copy *of Drab Interiors Monthly*. The mayor's office is on the second floor, adjacent to the Ceremonial Room. Probably the most beautiful room in the building, it is decorated with antique furniture, beautifully preserved hardwood floors, striking green marble, and a tasteful amount of gold leaf.

It would be in this room that we would announce to the world that Freddie Gray had died. We all gathered in the Executive Conference Room, with its connecting door to the Ceremonial Room. Surrounded by pictures of mayors past, it was a motley crew of citizens' groups, city officials, union officials, and police command staff. We were there for a singular purpose. To urge peace, to try and assuage any doubt or concern about the legitimacy of the investigation, and to make sure Baltimore didn't burn that night.

I have very little memory of what was said during the news conference. I've been tempted over the years to go back and watch the footage, but I haven't. There are a few moments that are as clear to me today as the day they happened. What I remember was looking at the lights on all the cameras. I remember thinking that each one of those cameras was going to make or break us. How the media carried our message would set the tone for the foreseeable future. I looked at the lights the whole time, almost in a fog. This was not the first time my agency had to announce an in-custody death. It was not the first time as the director of media relations that I had to organize such an announcement. This, though, in some esoteric, intangible way, felt very different.

I said to the police commissioner, shortly before we started, "This is our Ferguson." It was as much a prophetic warning as it was a sad resignation that all the work we had done, everything we had tried to do to really change the way we policed in Baltimore, was about to come to a crashing end. Left unspoken between us was the knowledge that a family was grieving. A community felt victimized, and there was little we could do to stop the coming tide.

CHAPTER 9

The National Media Arrives

Never let the truth get in the way of
a good story.

—MARK TWAIN

I don't really gamble. I don't have much of a poker face. The odd slot machine will keep me entertained in Vegas. The best gambling story I have took place on a Carnival Cruise ship in 2012. On a whim, I dropped $5 on the roulette table. I was passing through the casino (because you have to in order to get anywhere) and thought, why not? By some miracle of the gambling gods, I won a few rounds and walked away with $50. That was pretty cool. Later that night, the group I was with went back to the casino to continue celebrating a friend's birthday. I made mention that I had never played craps before, and off to the table we went.

I didn't have a clue what was happening. I was rolling the dice, and they were moving the money around. I knew I was doing well because we had attracted quite a crowd. I was just having fun. It felt very James Bond-like. I'm not sure how long I rolled for, but I do know I turned that original $50 into $6,000. And then I crapped out. All of it gone. I walked away from the table with everyone trying to console me. I didn't understand why they were upset. It had only cost me $5, and I had a great time.

That's sort of how I view the world in a lot of ways. Control the things you can control, accept those you cannot, and try to change things for the better whenever possible.

That experience aside, in reality, I shouldn't gamble. I don't have a poker face. Unless I am consciously thinking about my face, you can see everything I'm thinking like its splayed out on a big-screen television. My default facial expression is somewhere between "Why are you bothering me?" and "I hate everyone." I'm not really in a bad mood; it's just my default expression. I was thinking very carefully about my face on April 23. I was standing in front of City Hall doing a live interview with Jake Tapper from CNN.

I have a lot of respect for Mr. Tapper. He asks challenging questions, does a great deal of prep, and it shows. After several minutes of his questions that day, I was starting to get annoyed. He was asking me things that he knew I couldn't answer. He has had a long career as a reporter, and it wasn't the first time he'd covered a situation like this. Still, there he was, badgering away, asking me how it had happened and why we didn't have more answers. I get that. I do. It was his next statement, though, when I really had to think hard about my face. Through my earpiece, I heard him say, "…It's now eleven days later. It doesn't take eleven days to figure out what happened. If you gave me the six police officers, I could find out within an hour."

It was an utterly absurd thing for him to say. As he said it, I thought, "I know he didn't just suggest to me that we suspend the Constitution and beat the answer out of them."

I don't blame Jake Tapper for the question. It was not just him. This interview was indicative of all the interviews I had done the previous five days with national networks. At times, I felt like I was living in the studio that all of the networks tap into for their satellite interviews—a small, basement office located in downtown Baltimore, it became my second home as I, with incredible support from my team, attempted to keep the world informed about what was taking place on an almost minute-by-minute basis.

All of this media attention stemmed from two unavoidable circumstances. First, there was a national appetite for the information. Coming so closely on the heels of the Ferguson riots and then the Eric Garner protests in New York, the nation was already primed for another event. There is legitimate reason to cover an arrest and subsequent death of a person in police custody. The public certainly has a right to know about such an event. How that news is covered, responsibly or not, without bias or not, comes down to the outlet covering the story. Note that I said outlet, not reporter. Of the seemingly hundreds of reporters who were in Baltimore covering the events from April 12 through the early part of May, I can only think of a few who were there for "shock journalism." The vast majority of reporters wanted to tell the story the right way. Sadly, they were trapped in a corporate system that very often affects how the public receives their information.

Bernard Goldberg, a twenty-eight-year veteran of CBS News, wrote in his book, "Scaring the hell out of people makes for good TV, even when it makes for shallow journalism."[20] Nothing could better highlight the second, more disturbing, place a news organization gets its drive from: money. Money comes from advertisers, and advertisers pay more money to advertise on news programs with higher ratings. The more people you can get to watch your story, the more money you are going to make. This is a real and important aspect of how America digests news and information.

---

[20] Goldberg, Bernard. *Bias: A CBS Insider Exposes How the Media Distorts the News.* S.l.: Perennial, 2003.

A 2012 *Business Insider* article perfectly captured the issue with corporate control of the media. In 1983, about 90 percent of American Media was owned by fifty different companies. In 2011, that number had been consolidated to six. Just six companies in America own 90 percent of the media that the American consumer digests.[21] All of the major companies are beholden to stockholders to make money. Of course, you don't need me to tell you that different networks carry the news differently. Watch the same story covered on MSNBC and then Fox News and you will see the same story from diametrically opposed viewpoints, for the simple reason that they are catering to their audiences.

The divergent ways the media portrays stories was on full display in Baltimore. CNN had correspondents marching with the protesters asking them to share their past experiences with the BPD, while FOX News had their expert panels calling for more and more law enforcement officers to stop the protests from taking place. Note that I said protests, not riots. Depending on what network you were watching, you saw a very different version of the events taking place in the city.

This is a real problem when we talk about police reform. The issues that go into changing the dynamic of police-community interaction are complex and dynamic. There is no simple solution to the issue, and every side deserves the opportunity to have its voice heard without bias or influence. The national media will not stop covering police encounters the way they do until their viewers start demanding better. Sensationalism sells, hard stop. The more the story can be dramatized, the more it can emotionally connect, the more viewers will watch the story. The more viewers watch the story, the more money they make from advertising.

[21] Lutz, Ashley. "These 6 Corporations Control 90% Of The Media In America." *Business Insider*. June 14, 2012. https://www.businessinsider.com/these-6-corporations-control-90-of-the-media-in-america-2012-6.

All one had to do was look at how dramatically each of the three big cable news channels was covering the issues in Baltimore to see how dramatically coverage can be skewed to a viewing audience. While CNN was marching with protestors, Fox News was decrying the loss of civility and behavior. It was a deliberate effort to cater content to viewers, often ignoring facts to do so. Viewers demanding better will mean they have to step out of their confirmation bias: the need to seek information that conforms with their view of the world. It will mean being willing to look at the issues from all sides. It will also mean police departments have to start the work of connecting with their communities now, to equip them with the knowledge they need.

The media will play a critical role in perception of law enforcement for a long time to come. It is an important role, and in a free society, where the media is increasingly under attack, one that we should embrace. It is incumbent on all of us to demand truth and accuracy from our news sources. That doesn't mean hearing what we want to hear, or hearing what confirms our biases; it means we should be hearing the facts, for the sake of the facts.

We did what we could to get the facts out as accurately as we could. I was in the unique position of having an incredible team that supported me in those efforts. And I appreciate the card of thanks Mr. Tapper sent me, even if my name was spelled wrong.

CHAPTER 10

Violence Rocks Baltimore

Chaos was the law of nature;
Order was the dream of man.

—Henry Adams

In the days following Gray's death, my media appearances, especially with the national networks, became an unceasing round of interviews. Or so it seemed. This near omnipresence on the national stage resulted in a lot of mail being sent my way. Every day I was treated to my daily delivery of condemnation, vitriol, and quite a few letters letting me know precisely how the author intended to kill me. I even had a pastor from Connecticut write to tell me that he wasn't going to bother praying for my soul since it would be burning in hell. A wiser man would have likely taken these letters more seriously. I chalked them up to a public enraged over what was happening in Baltimore. Besides, I wasn't the first and certainly won't be the last police officer to be threatened with his or her own mortality.

What bothered me about the letters was that it was further proof our message wasn't getting out. It takes some degree of effort to handwrite or type out a letter, put it in an envelope with a stamp, look up our mailing address, and then get it to a post office, box, or mailing facility. It is easy to fire off an angry email or send a disparaging tweet; you have to really *want* someone to know how you feel to take the time to send a letter. And the more of them that came in, the more my impending sense of doom grew.

We had a brief decrease in the temperature in Baltimore. On April 20, it was clear that the news conference we had held the day before had not had the desired impact. A seething rage still needed to be addressed, so we decided to do another one the next day with the mayor and the police commissioner. Shortly before we went out, the commissioner was told by the lawyers at City Hall not to apologize and not to take responsibility. It was a legal decision. To do either of those things, in their view, would be to expose the city to great liability.

Commissioner Batts spoke first. In his remarks, he extended his heartfelt apology for the death of Freddie Gray, and he acknowledged that the Baltimore Police Department was at fault. He did this in direct contravention of the directive from the legal department. It was the best thing he could have done at the time. While legally sound, the advice was so contrary to the public good that there was no way he could follow it in good conscience. *Of course* we needed to apologize. This was a case in which a man had lost his life, and while we were beginning to acknowledge internally that it looked as if it was a horrible accident, we were still responsible. We also knew at that point that there had been a number of policy violations. How, with any degree of credibility, knowing beyond any measure of doubt that officers had violated our own policies, could he not accept responsibility? That was the true test of leadership: to do what was right, in the face of overwhelming animosity, because it was the right thing to do.

In a lot of ways, it was like releasing the pressure valve. People in the city were shocked by his acceptance of blame and responsibility. They saw a police department step up and openly acknowledge what we knew to be true. While it would ultimately cost the city $6.4 million in a settlement with the Gray family, it was exactly the right thing to do. Internally, the aphorism "lead balloon" doesn't do the response justice; this was also our fault.

There is a fine line that departments must walk when dealing with any issue involving officer conduct. Lean too heavily in favor of the community, and you lose your police officers. Lean too heavily in favor of the police officers, and you lose your community. This is the very essence of the problem. An officer can have done everything by policy, and by law, and still be wrong. The community can be outraged over an officer's conduct and still be wrong. Ed Flynn, who served as a police chief in three different departments, put it best at a conference a few years ago. In essence, he said we have gotten to a place in American society where people want to see police officers go to jail for policy failures, not violations of the law. We are in that place because, for too long, police departments haven't done a good job telling the community when and how we hold officers who are wrong accountable.

Therein lies the rub. Some internal investigations are long and complicated. When evaluating a dynamic situation, with the benefit of hindsight, it is easy to point out failings. What is critical, for legal and ethical reasons, is to conduct an investigation in a way that understands the officer's state of mind, with the knowledge they had (or should have had), at the time the incident unfolded. That can be a tricky thing to do. It takes time. In this age of immediate satisfaction (see Amazon two-hour delivery for proof) that is not a concept easily understood. Lengthy investigations appear as if the department is trying to cover up or conceal the facts. In reality, contrary to what you see on television, investigations can be slow and laborious. They can involve dozens and dozens of interviews, and then reinterviews, forensic analysis, toxicology reports (the results of which take ninety days on average to get back), video review, and on and on and on.

At the same time, there are cases in which you know within the first five minutes that the conduct was so glaringly out of compliance with policy, or against the law, that you know the officer was wrong. Yet, whatever the circumstances are, departments handle these situations exactly the same way. I would submit that is an outmoded and outdated way of operating. This will not be a popular statement to many police officers. I would challenge anyone to show me how this is the wrong approach. If the law enforcement profession can get to a place where it holds police officers accountable, publicly and quickly, when we know they are wrong, the converse will also be true. When you build that fundamental trust and credibility with your community by doing the right thing, then when you need the time to go through a complex investigation, earned trust and leeway will also be there. Here is the fundamental part of this argument: A police department derives its authority, its very existence, from the community it serves. It is incumbent on the profession to make that leap and create a better understanding.

Apologizing and taking responsibility was not an easy thing for Commissioner Batts to do that day. It was absolutely the right thing.

As the pressure in the city abated, if even a little, more and more activists, protestors, and concerned people from across the nation flooded into Baltimore. Some of these groups planned a protest march on Saturday, April 25, from Gray's arrest location to City Hall; 10,000 people were expected to attend.

We were good (really good) at these marches. Following the grand jury decision in New York regarding the death of Eric

Garner, Baltimore, like many major cities across the country, experienced days of protests, including some at which several hundred people marched through our streets. We learned very quickly how to keep the marches moving, how to connect with the group leaders, and how to keep the peace. We were one of the only major cities in the country not to make an arrest during any of those protest marches. My unit had also learned the value of embedding with reporters during these marches. My team would go out, and while I was in the watch center, they were with our local media to be able to provide immediate information and to prevent reporters from getting arrested by accident. It was a great system that worked well to keep the media and our public informed.

As a result of our earlier experiences in November and December, we were concerned about the march, but not overly so. What changed that thinking was intelligence that had been gathered about a specific subset of activists who were coming to Baltimore intent on causing chaos. Using social media to organize, groups like Anonymous promised chaos in Baltimore. In addition, there was concern about some of the organized gangs in Baltimore, notably the Bloods and Black Guerilla Family, and what role they would play. Ferguson was an example of activists traveling across the country and causing destruction. Social media is replete with examples of activist groups actively recruiting people to join their acts of destruction in Ferguson. The same thing was seen in New York during the marches to protest the grand jury decision in the wake of the death of Eric Garner. The combination of both organized and organic demonstrator groups had successfully caused chaos and destruction before. That wasn't going to happen here. We reached out to a number of departments in the state and asked for 1,000 additional police officers to supplement our officers who would be out on the streets to facilitate the peaceful march and protect critical infrastructure. Of the 1,000 police we asked for during the week, area departments agreed to send us 235 officers.[22] It was a far cry from what we asked for or what we needed.

Two things happened as a result of the sparse number of officers sent to the city. The first was an emergency meeting with regional representatives, held on April 24, begging for more assistance. During that meeting, the head of one of the police agencies present said, "I don't want my fucking patch to be on TV." The politics were real. We were unable to get area departments to send us more resources. Many of those present expressed the belief that nothing untoward would happen, that we were overreacting.

The second thing that took place was another news conference. In a much different tone from the one the preceding Monday, Commissioner Batts made clear that while we would do everything in our power to support peaceful protests, we would not allow any acts of violence or destruction to take place, and that we would do everything in our power to safeguard lives and property. The message internally and externally was clear: say what you want, march where you want, but you will be stopped if you hurt people or start to destroy property.

The march itself was incredibly peaceful. In lectures, I have described the march and subsequent rally at City Hall as something akin to a celebration of life. There were impassioned speakers, music, and criticism to be sure. But the tension that had been bubbling in the week between Gray's arrest and his death seemed to have ebbed away. It was as the last speaker was wrapping up that it changed in an instant. One of the leaders we had been most concerned about is known to march with a megaphone. Without warning, he picked up his megaphone and

---

[22] Baltimore Police Department. *2015 Civil Unrest: Looking Back—Moving Forward. Report.* 2015.

said, "Burn this motherfucker down." With that, what had been a largely peaceful protest morphed into a level of violence, chaos, and destruction not seen in more than forty years.

———•———

I was born in the wrong decade. The problem is, I'm not sure which is the right one. Depending on my mood, where I am, or what I'm listening to, there are always better options. *Back to the Future* lied—I want my hoverboard. There is something romantic about the 1920s, I love the style of the 1950s, and how I would want to be a fly on the wall during the American Revolution. My music taste is as varied as those decades. At any moment I might be listening to Vivaldi's Concerto in C Minor, Edith Piaf, or Billie Holiday singing anything, Samuel Barber's Adagio for Strings, or the latest Tiesto Remix. I would have danced at Studio 54, I would have been at every Puccini opening, and I would have been at Woodstock for the music.

Mid-Saturday afternoon, I was thinking about Woodstock as I walked out of BPD headquarters to take the short stroll to City Hall. I wanted to see firsthand how the protest gathering looked, and more importantly, what it felt like. I wanted to get a sense of the mood of the crowd, and it felt like what I imagine Woodstock would have felt like. Signs and music, people of all ethnicities, religions, social standing, gathered for a singular purpose. While the people gathered at Woodstock were there as part of the counterculture movement, the people gathered at City Hall had a much more intense purpose. They wanted their voices of frustration to be heard. They wanted someone to hear their cry. It was moving, peaceful, and brought a sense of hope that we might be at a bridge where we could truly start to have the conversation about what police reform should look like: a conversation where both police and community could express their concerns and look for a genuine path toward change.

Mixed in the crowd was a sinister, more extremist element. A few of them attempted to set an American flag on fire. The Guy Fawkes masks that have come to be synonymous with the Anonymous movement were everywhere, and there was no mistaking black-clad professional protestors (black bloc) who had come to Baltimore to sow dissension and chaos. I'd had enough intelligence briefings, and I had seen their antics in cities across the country; I knew what they were here for. They had no connection to Baltimore, no desire to see real change, nothing constructive to add to the equation: only chaos. My attention should have been focused on a different group who had come to wreak havoc, but for now, the black-clad interlopers had my attention.

After a short time, I returned to the watch center inside headquarters. I didn't see the end of the rally. I didn't hear the megaphone charge to burn the city down. I heard the radio transmission reporting it, and then on television and our own CCTV (closed-circuit television) feed, I saw what looked like hundreds of people running in the same direction, toward Camden Yards, where a baseball game was in progress with 30,000 people in the stadium. I watched in horror as that group of people began to assault people on the street, throw trash cans through windows, hurl rocks and debris at patrons outside the game, and then finally turn their aggression on the officers stationed at Camden Yards. Seeing people, faces unmasked, hurling bottles and rocks and metal barriers at officers wearing my uniform is a sight I will never forget. And I was filled with rage.

I detest knee-jerk reactions and broad-brush solutions. I much prefer to identify an issue and deal with it directly. Determine the cause, find a solution, implement the necessary remedy. As a proponent of police reform, that extends to officer conduct as well. If there is an officer who is wrong, apply the formula. If systematic change is needed, then do that as well. Don't respond with a knee-jerk reaction; that never fixes anything. To see officers who were at Camden Yards to keep fans safe attacked without distinction was infuriating beyond measure. They hadn't done anything to deserve what was happening to them. It had to stop.

Under normal circumstances, I would have stayed in the watch center, coordinating the public and media response to what was happening on national television. My unit, however, was incredibly short-staffed. I had to get on TV and start talking about what we were doing, how we were handling the situation, and urge calm. The only way to do that was to go to the cameras. So that's what I did.

Sergeant Jarron Jackson, Detective RaShawn Strong and I rushed to the scene, coordinating our arrival with the news desks. We didn't know we were about to get sucked into the action in an incredibly detrimental way. When I got to Lombard Street and Eutaw, a skirmish line was forming. Someone had relayed over the radio that a group was headed toward the firehouse at 15 South Eutaw Street, allegedly to steal the axes off of the trucks. I was the only commander on the scene at the time. Protecting the firehouse came first. So, I threw on my riot helmet, nodded at David Collins from WBAL, and with the assistance of the sergeants there, helped to organize the line and push the crowd back to the next block. Colonel Green arrived shortly thereafter, and I turned over command of the situation to him, took my helmet off and proceeded up to David's spot to get on camera. Boy, was that a mistake.

The first five minutes or so of the interview went well. David kept trying to pin me down about specifics and strategy. I kept defining our mission of ensuring a peaceful protest. At about the five-minute mark, I could hear the voices of protest coming toward me, and before I had a good sense of what was happening, I was surrounded by a group of about forty protestors. Watching the video, you can see my right hand below my waist, trying to wave over Detective Strong to come stand at my back. I was keenly aware that I was on live television and that anything I did that ran counter to the peaceful pronouncements I had been making would destroy the message we had been putting out. Other than the police commissioner, I was the most visible face of the agency. Anything that I did at this moment had the potential to cause devastating consequences for the department.

Before Detective Strong could get behind me, the first punch was thrown, hitting me in the upper back. In rapid-fire succession after the punch, someone threw part of a brick that hit me, and then one of the protestors swung a tree stake, striking me in the back. Detective Strong grabbed me, I grabbed David, and we pushed through the crowd. All of it was broadcast live.

I talk about this not because I want sympathy. In the following days, officers would endure far worse than I had. Truth be told, all three hits were largely absorbed by my ballistic vest. The issues this incident caused were far more dangerous than any momentary pain I may have experienced. The world just saw a uniformed police captain attacked on the air. That would set the tone for the rest of the night. In several subsequent standups David did after the attack, he held up either part of the brick I had been hit with or the stake and talked about them. That did severe damage to our public statements. My job was to define the events of the day, not to be a part of them.

The more immediate concern for me was that we lost our ability to communicate effectively for the remainder of the day. Clearly, being on the street, going on camera was no longer an option. I was ordered, tersely, back to headquarters. No one was happy about

84

seeing me assaulted on television, and they didn't want a repeat. To be fair, neither did I. However, our entire communication strategy for television was built around being on the street and going live as needed. We had no plans for a media staging area at Headquarters, and because of the massive security footprint around the building, it would have been a logistical nightmare to escort each camera crew in and out for briefings. In essence, we lost our ability to be on television through a lack of preplanning and limited staffing.

I can't describe in great detail what the rest of the day was like. I have read the after-action reports, and I've watched countless hours of coverage on YouTube. The rest of that day, for me, was spent in a six-foot by six-foot office off of the command post. I would call one station, start talking on the air about what was going on for a few minutes, hang up, call the next one, and repeat. While I was talking, Detective Jeremy Silbert was sitting across from me live-tweeting everything I was saying. Jackson and Strong were running me little pieces of paper from the watch center, telling me where the crowd was, how we were responding, and everything else that was taking place.

It wasn't ideal, but it was what we had. A critical component of effective crisis communication is to be able to project calm and candor and to break the flow of images on the screen with frequent briefings. I wasn't able to do that. Now I was trapped in a room and losing the information war. I take full responsibility for that failure. I should have had a backup plan, and I didn't. We did the best we could, but with thousands of officers counting on me to make sure Baltimore saw their heroic efforts, I failed them. It would not be the only failure of the day.

By just about any metric upon which you could judge the BPD we, the senior command, failed the people of Baltimore, and as importantly, our own officers. The destruction caught all of us by surprise. Violence from a protest simply wasn't something that happened in Baltimore, and we had not adequately prepared. I don't mean in the moment; there were lots of errors there. But as an organization, we had not invested the proper amount of time in incident command training, crowd enforcement techniques, or properly equipping our officers. These efforts should have started years prior, but our focus had been on the almighty homicide number.

All of the independent after-action reports and BPD's internal report showed dramatic systemic and systematic failures that endangered our officers and the people of Baltimore. I also take full responsibility for my part in this failure. I had never envisioned that this was the path we would head down, at least not like this. I was supposed to be one of the forward-looking people in the organization, and I didn't live up to that expectation. Others in command must do their own soul-searching about what happened that day.

I've had a lot of people tell me that it would have been impossible to predict the events that would unfold on April 25 and that we handled it better than could be expected. That simply is not good enough. Officers were hurt, businesses were damaged, and a city was paralyzed with fear over what had just happened.

Part of being a good leader is not only accepting or acknowledging the mistakes that you make but also taking responsibility for them. The events that unfolded on April 25 were traumatic, disorienting, dangerous, and unacceptable. They also exposed a vital weakness in our response to violent protests. That exposure would set the tone for what was to come.

CHAPTER 11

The Prelude to More Violence

*Memory is deceptive because it is
colored by today's events.*

—ALBERT EINSTEIN

O ne of the greatest blessings I have in my life is my memory.
I have a wonderful ability to absorb information and recall
it, for the most part, when I need it. I'm the guy you don't
want to play Trivial Pursuit with. I have a vast collection of
absolutely useless information that rattles around in my head
like a game of *Jeopardy* gone mad.

Once during a command staff meeting, for reasons that baffle
me, I found myself regaling the assembled commanders with the
how the British royal family came to be known as the Windsors.
With as much excitement as I had once told my family about
Pluto, I told everyone in the room the tale of the decline of the
Stuart line, leading to the importation of the Hanoverian George
I as king, leading to his descendants assuming the throne, leading
to Queen Victoria marrying Prince Albert of Saxe-Coburg and
Gotha, leading to King George V changing the name to Windsor
at the outbreak of World War I. It was about halfway through
this glorious rendition that I realized three things: No one in the
room cared, my inner geek was on full display, and that there
was no way I was going to stop until I got to the end. A self-

diagnosed Anglophile, I knew this tidbit of knowledge was clearly important to whatever we were talking about. At least in my mind.

I relate all of that to say this: it is with great frustration that I can't remember April 26… at all. It's like a really wide paintbrush wiped my memory with the darkest of paints to remove all knowledge of the events that transpired that day. I've thought about this a lot. In hindsight, to a degree it makes sense. I had spent weeks not sleeping. We were so busy, there was so much going on, I had been averaging two to three hours of sleep a night since April 13. I was living off enormous cans of Monster energy drink, with quad venti Starbucks anything getting me through to the next can of Monster. I'm fairly certain that my heart actually got to work before I did, so amped up on caffeine; surely it jogged to work faster than I could drive. I was blowing through three cell phone batteries a day, even keeping my phone attached to a charger. The media never stopped, the meetings never stopped, the planning never stopped, the conference calls never stopped. Each day felt like I was lurching from one critical moment to the next.

My limited staff— Sarah Connolly, Jarron Jackson, Jeremy Silbert, RaShawn Strong, and Dale Wood—were all equally exhausted. Pam Barnes, affectionately referred to as Ms. Pam, our office assistant, kept us moving and as organized as she could. The worst part was that there was seemingly no end in sight. Humans have an amazing ability to push themselves through to reach goals that appear out of reach. Determination, grit, and perseverance are hallmarks of successful individuals. What makes it possible is the knowledge that there is a goal to achieve; there is a finish line. Each subsequent day after April 12 compounded the sense that there was no finish line; it would just get worse each day. More protestors would arrive, and their agitation would grow. More media would arrive, and their questions would become more intense. The goalpost we couldn't see kept getting moved. There is a phrase, "the fog of war," that is utterly appropriate for what it felt like to be in the midst of everything that was going on.

Lissa Druss and Judy Pal were life preservers, just enough to keep me afloat. Every day I called each one of them. They are remarkably similar, and yet so very different. Their guidance and insight were critical to each and every day. Lissa is a Chicagoan, in every sense of the word. She is ridiculously smart, stylish, has a smile that would stop traffic, and a personality that is as joyful as it is blunt. A renowned public relations strategist and publicist, she had an award-winning career as a journalist before becoming a consultant. After one news conference, she called me and said, "What the hell are you doing? Stop holding your notes so low. You look like an idiot." It was like manna from heaven having a clear voice to tell me all the things I couldn't see. Judy, having left the department about a year-and-a-half prior, was more nuanced in her critique, but no less powerful. "Eric, you did great; stop saying 'so' before you answer every question." It wasn't just their critiques of my performance that was vital. They offered me a chance to sound out strategy, to see things with fresh eyes, and to challenge my assumptions. They weren't afraid to tell me when I was wrong or to offer suggestions about how to be more successful. Our daily conversations were a short oasis from chaos.

No one has all the answers. Anyone who says they do is someone not to be trusted. I certainly didn't have all the answers, and I will forever owe each of them a debt I can never repay. Commissioner Batts had taught me the value of listening to everyone. Now I was putting it into practice during an ongoing onslaught of crisis and confusion. I don't say any of this to sound hyperbolic. This situation was real and had the potential to be deadly. We had officers who were injured, police cars set on fire, businesses that had been looted, and we knew it was only going to get worse as we approached Gray's funeral.

What I do know about that Sunday, having compiled the internal review, is that an urgent request was once again sent out to the state for more assistance on Monday. Monday would be Gray's funeral, and if Saturday had shown us anything, it was that events could spiral out of control with alarming speed. We needed help. Again, we asked for an additional 1,000 police officers from around the state to come in and assist us. We were no longer being hyperbolic in our assumptions of what could happen. It had happened. The violence was real, the destruction was real, the injuries were real.

We also had intelligence that a "purge" was being planned for Mondawmin Mall following Gray's funeral. Taking the name from the movie franchise, the idea was to create a lawless environment of violence and destruction. The message was spreading virally across social media. Taken from the BPD's after-action report, the Analytical Intelligence Unit stated:

> At approximately noon on Sunday, the Intelligence Analysis Unit reported to Unified Command and Watch Center Commanders that there were social media rumors of a potential juvenile "purge" occurring on Monday, April 27, 2015 at 3:00pm "from Mondawmin, to the Ave (North Ave), (and) back to downtown." A confidential source identified the poster as ███████████.[23] His information, as well as the flier he posted was disseminated to the Baltimore City School Police. School Police were asked to provide intelligence Monday when they reported to Unified Command on what had occurred

---

[23] Redacted for security and privacy reasons.

at schools during the day. At this time the intelligence was deemed credible. In addition to Unified Command, Watch Center Commanders, and School Police, the Maryland Transportation Authority Police Department and the Operational Intelligence Section were also notified of the possible event and the original poster's information.

Surely help would come. But once again, politics are real.

CHAPTER 12

The Riot Seen around the World

A riot is the language of the unheard.

—Martin Luther King Jr.

P olice have a lot of slang, and most of it is regional. One of the terms batted about is a "radio ear." In short, it is the ability to almost subconsciously listen to the radio while carrying on a phone call, talking to someone in person, or singing along to your favorite song in the car; everyone does it, even police. "Radio ear" is an amazing trait. I'm assuming it's like what a mother does when she has kids. You know when to tune out the noise and when it matters. Nothing cuts through distractions faster than the tone of voice an officer gets when they're in trouble. It's easy to hear when someone is yelling or screaming; most times, it's more subtle. It's a change in voice, hard to describe, yet instantly recognizable. It will make you stop in your tracks to listen—you'll cut off a conversation mid-word. Nothing is more important than that radio transmission.

When it is an officer who truly needs help, nothing will make you move faster or your heart beat harder as adrenaline courses through your body. You can never get there fast enough as heart soul, mind, and body merge to will yourself to already be on the scene to help. It is almost as if every atom in your body, driven by its own will, propels you toward the sound. One voice in distress is enough to make your blood run cold. When it's seemingly hundreds of voices, you can feel your whole world slip away in a chasm of angst and fear so deep and so wide it engulfs you with sorrow and rage.

Standing in the watch center on the afternoon of April 27, that is exactly what happened to me. *We* were under attack. *We* were being hurt and injured. *Our* city was descending into anarchy. Every molecule in my body screamed at me: "*Move!*" As officer after officer keyed up their radios calling for help, the urge became nearly overwhelming. At one point, I had actually started for the door when the chief of staff locked her hands on my shoulders, telling me to stay where I was. Tears of frustration, anger, sadness filled my eyes. I understood why she held me in place; she did the right thing. But for that one moment, I had never hated anyone more in my life.

"We're getting fucking slaughtered out here, send us help, *now!*" came the plea from one of the commanders on scene. Rocks the size of oranges hurtled through the air, missiles aimed at my fellow officers. Chunks of concrete and bricks came next, a salvo of debris launched with the singular intent of injuring, maiming, maybe even killing an officer. The call of "officer down" reverberated through the watch center like an explosion. More and more of those calls came in as officers were injured, some seriously, by the ceaseless onslaught. I watched in abject horror as our armored vehicle, sent in to rescue officers who were so injured they couldn't move, came under attack. Within a matter of minutes, its windows were completely shattered. So great was the power of the attack that a vehicle designed to withstand gunshots was rendered virtually useless in a matter of moments.

As these images played out on television, more and more people from the surrounding areas joined in the attack. And then it spread from west to east across the city. Like any riot in human history, the reason that people join in varies as much as they do. Some just wanted to be a part of the action. Some people came to loot. Undoubtedly, there were those who were swept up by the emotions of the day. And there were those for whom decades of frustration manifested in this singular torrent of visceral emotion. The scar had been ripped open and, like a dam breaking, those who felt that their concerns, their voices, their cry had never been heard, exploded in a melee of violence.

It didn't matter that I wasn't there. I felt every hit in my soul. Call after call for help, image after image of rioting tore at the dream and hopes I had for a peaceful resolution. With every second that ticked by, I was filled with a palpable sense of dread that everything we had worked for was dying. I had not used enough of the right words, I hadn't convinced enough people, I hadn't done enough to stop what was happening. I had let down each of the officers, and their families, and the people of Baltimore. I had failed. No one had heard my cry.

—•—

Like a lot of other commanders in the department, I started the morning of April 27 worried about how the day would unfold. The violence we had seen on Saturday had been shocking, to say the least. Our haphazard response showed that systematically, we were not prepared for large-scale acts of violence. The surrounding agencies in the state had not sent us the resources we knew we needed, our incident command structure had failed miserably, the lack of any real crowd-control training was evident, and there was a palpable sense that everything was about to go sideways.

Based on the intelligence gathered on Sunday, we again put out a request for 1,000 additional police officers to supplement the officers we were already deploying. There was too much ground to cover, and Saturday had been a visceral lesson in how quickly things can go wrong. Freddie Gray's funeral was about to take place, and we knew that chaos was surely to follow. We didn't get the 1,000 officers we asked for. Not even close. In fact, by the end of the day, we would only have an additional 250 officers on the streets of Baltimore. I have no explanation for why we didn't receive the support we so desperately needed. I can speculate about the role of interpersonal relationships and political motivations, but speculation is not proof. What I do know is that with evidence in hand that a "purge" was planned, we had nowhere near the assistance we needed.

The Commissioner was in my office early in the morning, and we were talking about what communications would look like that day. In the midst of the conversation, the commander of the Criminal Intelligence Unit came in. He provided us a quickly drawn-up intelligence summary. That summary and our response to it would become one of the more hotly contested decisions that we made that day. The Baltimore City Fraternal Order of Police, Lodge Number 3, specifically criticized me in their report for how we handled the information we were given. What they didn't take into account was the lessons we had learned from New York.

———•———

On December 20, 2014, a man named Abdullah Brinsley shot his girlfriend in the stomach in Owings Mills, Maryland. After shooting her, he drove to New York, sending out social media messages on the way. In those messages, he made clear his intent to kill police officers. Baltimore County Police sent a warning to NYPD; sadly, it arrived too late. Just after 2:45 p.m., Brinsley carried out his threat, murdering Officers Rafael Ramos and Wenjian Liu in cold blood. He shot them from behind as they sat in the patrol car. It was a murder that shocked the nation and solidified the narrative within law enforcement circles that we were under attack.

One of the criticisms leveled at Baltimore County Police was that their warning had been too little, too late. Only a few months later, we were faced with a similar warning and a question of what to do with it.

The report was stark and clear. An informant had alerted his contacts inside the BPD that he had information about a gang meeting he had witnessed. He claimed that he had direct knowledge of a meeting between members of the Bloods, Crips, and Black Guerilla Family, wherein each gang had vowed to kill a BPD officer on the day of Gray's funeral as retribution. The informant also provided the detectives with information that we hadn't released to the public: He knew where certain individuals had been hiding guns in preparation for the act. Over the previous days, a number of guns had been hidden on rooftops in the city, and this activity had been observed through various surveillance methods. Based on the informant's previous interaction with our detectives and the additional information about the guns, the Criminal Intelligence Unit determined this threat to be credible. All of this information was detailed in their after-action report, pieces of which ended up in the BPD's own internal after-action report. The informant had been transported to the FBI Field Office in Woodlawn, Maryland for further debriefing.

Faced with this information, the police commissioner made the decision to make the information known to as many people as possible. It was put into intelligence briefings for officers who would work that day. An alert was sent out to agencies in the area. And I put out a news release at the request of the police commissioner. There would be a lot of officers coming into the city that day who wouldn't be at our briefings, and we wanted to make sure as many people were aware of the threat as possible. Coming on the heels of the horrendous incident in New York, it only made sense.

There was a lot of speculation at the time, including in the Fraternal Order of Police's report, that this decision to make the information public exacerbated the situation. In the coming days, the city council president would march with gang leaders, calling the report ridiculous. The FBI would later say the information was unsubstantiated. I want to make one point about that. They didn't say that it was a false report or that our assessment was incorrect; they simply said they didn't have enough information to verify the report. I'll leave the judgment used by the city council president to march with gang members to minds more intelligent than mine. What I do know with certainty is that to say it exacerbated the situation is to look for something to blame, beyond the obvious. The flyers calling for a "purge" were already circulating. The table had already been set.

What I do know now is what I knew then. After all the reviews, all the reports, the analysis is the same. To not release the information would have been grossly negligent. Hard stop. Even if we hadn't put it out publicly, it would have leaked. Too many people had their hands on the information. To allow a threat like that to leak in an uncontrolled manner would have only added fuel to the fire and caused speculation that we were purposely trying to mislead the public. Blaming the report conveniently ignores the fact that we had already seen violence on Saturday. It ignores the documented influence of outside groups that had come into Baltimore to sow seeds of violence. It also provides an easy out. Blaming the report meant not having to take a hard look at the decades-long policies—or lack thereof—that had placed us in this moment.

———•———

Shortly after we put out the news release describing the intelligence assessment, Gray's funeral began. An eerie truce descended on the city. It was a far different feeling than the previous Saturday. Rather than the near-celebratory nature of that afternoon, this was a tense, fragile, and soon-to-be-fleeting peace. Anyone who has ever gone through a tornado knows the feeling. The air gets heavier, your senses heighten, and instinctively you know something bad is about to happen. I found myself bouncing back and forth between my office to answer inquiries and the watch center to get updates about our deployment and the latest intelligence we had acquired. The funeral was televised, but I couldn't watch. The silent war raging in the back of my brain needed to be isolated. I didn't need the emotions of a funeral to cloud my thinking. I could be human later. For now, I felt the need to be prepared.

I had finally settled in the watch center, standing next to the chief of staff. The police commissioner was out on the street to see the deployment at Mondawmin Mall. Lieutenant Colonel Melissa Hyatt was in charge. While there were two deputy police commissioners and the chief of patrol floating in and out of the watch center, no one was more qualified to be in command. The first female SWAT team leader in the department's history, she had a tremendous amount of experience organizing and responding to crowd-control situations. Hyatt is also the perfect blend of grace under fire, intelligence beyond measure, and an absolute command presence that make her a force to be reckoned with. I have no doubt that she will lead a police department one day, and they will be better for having her.

It is not an easy thing to be a woman in law enforcement. It is still an overwhelmingly male-dominated profession. Most reporting puts the figure of women in law enforcement around 13 percent.

The majority of that percentage work in urban organizations.[24] For Hyatt to have achieved all that she has in her career is a testament to her own personal fortitude. She never played the political game, and she didn't ask for special treatment. Rather, she wanted to be treated as an equal and worked her ass off to rise through the department.

I had just finished saying something to her when it happened. It was like a blur. Mondawmin Mall, the largest mall in the city, also happened to be the largest transit hub in the city. From the video link the police helicopter *Foxtrot* was providing, you could see the crowd of teenagers surge toward the officers. They already had rocks in their hands. We would later learn that several of them had gotten off of busses with their backpacks preloaded with rocks to throw. They began to pelt officers who had been sent to keep the peace. Without warning, the crowd began to swell as people emptied out of their houses and the mall to join in the fray. The number of people who were there just seemed to grow exponentially.

Chaos erupted in the watch center. Lt. Col. Hyatt was attempting to orchestrate the response as other commanders began to shout over her. Multiple people were giving conflicting orders on the radio. The screams and shouts for help began to pour in from the scene. Within seconds, we were witnessing a full-blown riot. Officers were being injured as their riot shields shattered under the onslaught of the rocks and bricks. Those hit in the head would see their helmets fracture on impact. At one point, the armored vehicle was sent in to rescue officers who couldn't walk. All four windows, designed to withstand gunfire, were shattered by the ceaseless barrage. A row of houses that was under renovation supplied ample ammunition, with pallets of bricks to choose from.

---

[24] "Women in Law Enforcement." Secret Service Duties, Past, Present, & Future. Accessed September 02, 2018. http://www.criminaljusticeschoolinfo.com/women-law-enforcement.html.

CHAPTER 12

As the chaos on the streets grew, so did the chaos in the watch center. There was an all-out screaming match taking place. Confusion and panic gripped those charged with making the decisions necessary to protect those on the street. Despite the swirling sea of confusion, Hyatt remained calm. A steely tone I had never heard her use came across the radio as she tried to send in additional resources to supplement the officers on the street. At one point, two of the most senior people in the department walked out of the room, completely abdicating their responsibility to those being hammered with bone-shattering debris. One would be found later in his office, hiding from the world.

More and more officers arrived on scene only to be met with the same slew of concrete and bricks that had all but broken the first wave of officers. Still, in a perfect example of courage and bravery, the line of officers never broke. They never retreated. Those images of bravery should be what people remember: officers who didn't know the people who were attacking them, or the people they were protecting, standing shoulder-to-shoulder against all odds to put down a riot. They are heroes. Period.

It must seem that I'm contradicting myself. How could they be heroes? I've been advocating for the need for law enforcement to reform, I talked about this being our due, and I agree with Dr. King: a riot is the cry of the unheard. That doesn't mean I support anarchy. Nor does it mean that the people who lived in that neighborhood, who were rightly terrified, deserved what was happening to them. It doesn't mean the small business owners should have had their livelihood smashed and burned to the ground. This was destruction for the sake of destruction. All this would do is galvanize the resolve on both sides that they were morally superior. That would make meaningful reform that much harder.

Then the chaos began to spread. Reports were coming in of rioters moving toward North Avenue and Pennsylvania Avenue, only a few short blocks from the mall and the location where Freddie Gray had first been observed before his arrest on April 12. Soon we started receiving calls that rioters were now on the east side of the city. With each new report, the insanity that was taking place in the watch center only grew. Too much noise, too many conflicting orders and confusion had now taken over. Entire platoons of officers who had been staged around the city couldn't be raised on the radio. Much-needed equipment was stuck in traffic and couldn't get to where it was needed. The confusion was only amplified with allied agencies, which had little or no radio communication with the watch center. There is no way to know if this confusion allowed the initial incident to spread, or if a better-coordinated response could have contained what was happening. Other events would later indicate that it couldn't have been stopped in those first few moments. Nonetheless, the initial response was dismal, and far from what the people of Baltimore, and the officers of the Baltimore Police Department, deserved.

Throughout the beginning of the riot, I was standing in my corner of the room. Watching it all unfold, I was partly ashamed by what I was witnessing, mostly feeling the sickening sense that I had failed. I felt hot tears of rage fill my eyes and fought to keep my composure. The radio calls were punches to my soul. The overwhelming urge to get to the line and help was primal. It was in this moment that the chief of staff grabbed my shoulders and reminded me I had a job to do. It was the wakeup call I needed. Pulling out my nearly dead cell phone, I called the commissioner and uttered one sentence: "You need to get back here right now."

"Got it," was the response, and I hung up.

It would be easy to assume that Hyatt lost control of the room. Nothing could be further from the truth. She was the one person who remained calm and tried to get desperately needed help to the officers under attack. What was painfully apparent, however, was that years of focusing just on the homicide number meant that in this moment, the support she needed didn't have the training or experience necessary to provide it—a fact that was clearly highlighted in the Police Executive Research Forum (PERF) report that would come later.

Murphy's Law dictates, "Whatever can go wrong will go wrong." It did. In the midst of everything that was happening the video downlink with, the police helicopter *Foxtrot* failed, and we lost our eyes in the sky. We were now operating blind. For several minutes, we tried unsuccessfully to reestablish the link, but it was clear the issue would not be easily resolved. While technicians were working on the fix, Commissioner Batts walked into the room and began to reestablish some sense of order. I called Tanya Black at WJZ, a local television outlet, and said, "Tanya, we need your helicopter."

Without skipping a beat, she said, "Just tell me where." It was an incredible gesture of cooperation and generosity, one for which I will always be thankful. For the next thirty minutes or so, the images that were shown on WJZ weren't chosen in a news control room; they came from us.

A 911 call came in for North Avenue and Pennsylvania Avenue, in the middle of the block, describing a desperate situation. The one officer who was available was sent to investigate. When the officer exited his patrol vehicle, groups that had been hiding in the alleys on either side of the street emptied out into the block, charging toward the officer. He retreated into an open doorway, holding the crowd back at gunpoint. They then turned and attacked the officer's patrol car, ripping the doors open, smashing the windows, and ravaging the interior. In the midst of this, we received a second 911 call stating that we had an officer who had been killed at that location. We had WJZ fly their helicopter to that location, and the image on the scene sent shockwaves through the room. A large crowd of people were on and in the car. Both the driver and passenger doors had been folded backward. The windows were smashed out, and we believed we had a dead officer in the car.

The police commissioner ordered a deputy commissioner and several platoons to the location, saying "They will not drag the body of one of our officers through the streets." It was a surreal thing to hear. Images of Somalia flooded my head, and I wondered how far we had fallen. It would only be much, much later that we would find out the officer was OK. This was the mood and understanding of what was taking place as the riot began to unfold.

Deputy Police Commissioner Dean Palmere arrived on the scene and began to form the responding officers into a skirmish line when the first explosion ripped through the intersection. A series of timer-driven improvised explosive devices (IEDs) had been planted around the intersection. They were timed perfectly with the response of our backup officers to the 911 call of an officer who had been killed. The Baltimore Police Department was under a coordinated, sustained attack, and we didn't know it.

Brian Keubler from WMAR would later produce one of the only stories highlighting the IEDs that were used.[25] Propane canisters had been rigged with rudimentary timers, including charcoal, and were placed around the intersection. Purchased at Walmarts

[25] "BREAKING: Baltimore PD Confirms IED In Monday's Riots." Truth Revolt. April 29, 2015. Accessed September 10, 2018. https://www.truthrevolt.org/news/breaking-baltimore-pd-confirms-ied-mondays-riots.

around the city, they were placed well in advance of the initial outbreak of violence at the Mondawmin Mall. One of them caused the library on North Avenue to catch on fire. By the grace of God, no one was killed or injured by the devices. They did stop our forward momentum in gaining control of the riot as it continued to spread across West (and now East) Baltimore.

Those who say that the news release concerning the alleged gang threat caused the riot have little to say about how that release led to an attack involving IEDs. Riots build on themselves. All that is needed is a small group of people to get the ball rolling. While Freddie Gray's death was the spark that ignited the fire, the larger inferno was planned. The initial rioters came armed with rocks and chunks of concrete. The location was chosen because of the houses that were under construction, providing a tremendous amount of additional ammunition. People were hiding in an alley and lured an officer to that location for the purpose of pulling more officers into an intersection filled with IEDs.

Of course, these facts do not take away from the reasons we arrived here in the first place. They do not alleviate the need to reform the profession. However, as history remembers the events of April 27, 2015, it is important to remember that the riot itself was a planned, coordinated, and orchestrated attack.

CHAPTER 13

Baltimore Burns

*It is during our darkest moments that we
must focus to see the light.*

—ARISTOTLE

W hen I was eight, I nearly drowned. My family was on vacation in Saint Lucia, staying on the Atlantic side of the island, which has stronger currents than the Caribbean side. My brother and I were in the ocean, playing in the waves. From before I have memory, my mom had us swimming. She is a competitive swimmer herself, and spending time in the water has always been a fundamental part of my life. Even today, I refuse to live anywhere that isn't close to water. Of course we were in the water; it was the only place we would be.

Mom came out and was swimming with us. I distinctly remember the tone of panic that poured out of her mouth as she screamed hold on, grabbing my brother and me. We didn't see the wave that she had seen coming. Strong and powerful, it drove us into the seabed. Even now, I can feel the sand, bead-sized pebbles that ripped into my skin. I can remember the swirl of colors as sunlight filtered by the water mixed with the honey-colored sand flashed across my eyes as we tumbled in the wave. The utter confusion I experienced as push became pull and I felt myself being dragged backward. Through it all, my mother never let go.

I will never understand the herculean feat of strength that she mustered to hold onto to two children in a brutal undercurrent. I blacked out in the water, waking up on the beach sputtering water and crying. Even as a child, fear was never something that I let overwhelm me. As soon as we were able, back into the water we went. It has been a lifelong love affair.

As I grew older, two important life lessons developed out of that experience. One, we are powerless against the wave. It will knock you down, rip your skin, steal the oxygen from your lungs, and leave you a broken, sobbing mess. The second was that, provided you didn't die, then you get up and do it again. You fight against the wave, you stand your ground, you figure out a better way to take the hit, and after much trial and error, you find yourself on your feet.

As shock and horror over what I was seeing began to recede, I felt the wave coming.

The emotions of the moment on April 27 gave way to a steely determination that this moment would not define my department, my city, or my beloved profession. We would push through, we would put the riot down, we would protect our city, and I would define for the world what they were seeing. Baltimore would not be the next Ferguson.

As officers fought with rioters who were smashing and burning everything in sight, I prepared my own battle. This was the moment national and international media had been waiting for. Quite simply, this made for great TV. I instructed my team to gather media for a briefing in our staging area and I jumped on the phone with as many stations as I could reach to start countering the narrative they were forming. Yes, there was a riot; it was violent and destructive. Hundreds of people had been injured by this point, and Mondawmin Mall was being looted. Fires were springing up in East and West Baltimore, and officers from across the region were rushing toward the city to assist. Still, it wasn't the whole city. Hundreds of thousands of Baltimoreans were in their homes or offices watching what was happening. They needed to know we were doing everything we could to protect their city, our city, as did the families of all of the officers who were in harm's way, and they needed to know that we were going to do everything in our power to keep their loved ones safe.

We activated the plan we had used Saturday afternoon while we waited for the media to gather. Time had a malleable quality to it. Everything seemed to be moving around us faster than it was possible to comprehend, and yet it felt as if we were moving through molasses. The images on the screen were vibrant, palpable, visceral. Here was a shot of people running in and out of a CVS they were looting, with a police car engulfed in flames in front of it. There was a shot of firefighters attempting to put out a blaze with rioters slashing at the hoses with knives. Next an image of officers, lined shoulder to shoulder, as concrete and bricks were hurled at them, they in turn deploying smoke canisters to disperse the growing crowds. There was no way my voice alone would be enough. It was time to get on TV.

Speaking for the Baltimore Police Department for the last two-and-a-half years had given me tremendous experience in front of cameras. I had worked hard to hone my craft. Use the right tone of voice, keep a neutral face, ensure that our message gets out. In all that time, through all of the scandal and conflict, joy and success that I talked about with news crews, I always had been careful about how I carried myself. I wasn't representing me; I was speaking for the Office of the Police Commissioner, and the women and men who were wearing the badge. I was merely the conduit for the message. This time would be different. A carefully presented message wouldn't cut through the noise and trauma currently being shown on every channel I turned to.

I walked up to the commissioner right before I got on the elevator to go brief the media and asked, "How do you want me to be?"

His response caught me off guard. "How do you feel right now?"

Without thinking, I replied, "I'm pretty fucking pissed."

"Go be that way on TV," came the verdict. And that's how I found myself on the elevator ride down. That sense that I was about to get knocked down by the wave was intense. I have talked about what it was like to go down the elevator and through the lobby on the way to brief the cameras. I have said before it was arguably the most important briefing I ever held in my career. There are things I wish I had done differently during that briefing. Hindsight is always 20/20. In that moment, though, I let my heart lead.

After the news conference was over, I returned to the watch center and experienced what is likely the most bizarre moment of the entire day. Everyone stood up and started clapping. It was uplifting, embarrassing, reassuring, and likely a much-needed, stress-relieving outlet for everyone in the room. I had never had one of my news conferences reviewed in real time before. Selfishly, it was the boost I needed to continue to face the media for the rest of the day. It might seem odd to have all this emotion wrapped around a press briefing. Stop for a moment and imagine that you are going to speak to a room of 100 people, without prepared remarks, on a subject that has just been given to you. Now imagine that the words you use can determine what that room thinks about you, all your coworkers, and the place that you live. That can be a little intimidating, right? Now, imagine the same situation, only instead of 100 people, it's tens of millions of people. The wave had hit, and I was still standing, albeit on shaky legs.

———•———

For nearly four hours, the officers of the BPD and the few officers from outside agencies who were already in the city battled the rioters. It was an ebb and flow of taking and losing ground— pushing the crowds down one street only to have them loop back on another. Somewhere in the midst of this battle, the mayor and her staff arrived. They moved into a small office off the watch center's main floor, where conversation about declaring a state of emergency continued in earnest. It might seem like this would be a simple decision; nothing could be further from the truth. It is a complex decision with political, financial, and civil liability. It is also a public acknowledgment that things have spiraled out of control. This is not a position any elected official wants to be in, especially in a situation in which the emotional cost is so high.

Baltimore is a "home rule" city, and the mayor would have to declare a state of emergency for the governor to send in additional resources, including the National Guard. In the short term, that would bring immediate assistance. In the long term, what would be the consequences for the city? What would be the impact of having armed military troops on the streets of Baltimore? What would that do to a population that already felt under siege? What message would be sent to the officers of the BPD about their ability to handle the situation? This riot might have been planned, but it only existed because of the emotions of the day. How you balance all the conflicting aspects of a riot is tricky business, indeed.

A lot of criticism was leveled at Mayor Stephanie Rawlings-Blake during and after the Freddie Gray Riots. To view her or her actions solely through the lens of the media narrative is to miss a much greater aspect of who she is and how she governed. There is blame to go around; I certainly accept my failures, and as mayor, she certainly is entitled to her fair share of criticism. To criticize her failures without acknowledging her successes, however, is to push a narrative that is jaded at best.

Mayor Stephanie Rawlings-Blake was never one to shy away from controversy. She made Baltimore one of the first sanctuary cities in America, implemented controversial and much-needed fiscal policies at the height of the great recession, and enacted reform measures with public safety pensions that all but made her a sworn enemy of police in Baltimore. Eight years later, there is still a raging lawsuit over that decision. She also built the first new recreation centers in a generation, secured a AAA bond rating for the first time in the city's history, performed the first gay marriage in the city, and still is a fierce advocate for those who don't have equal treatment. During her tenure, she had to deal with a historic blizzard, an earthquake, a derecho, a tornado, flooding, and a hurricane. She also believes in the nobility of law enforcement while at the same time being very aware that the profession needs to change to better serve communities.

In other words, she is not afraid to take steps to do what she believes to be the right thing, even if it's not the popular thing. You could ask for far worse in a leader. Sadly, in today's world of immediate gratification and an ongoing narrative that those who don't think like you are your enemies, her actions often created controversy. I have spent a lot of time wondering if, as a people, we were more willing to talk and listen, how controversial would she really be? Perhaps the reason she engendered so much animosity is that she did what she said she was going to do. She didn't try to appease special interests; rather, she tried to do the right thing, at the right time, in the wrong environment.

On April 25, shortly after the first incident of violence, the mayor held a news conference to urge peace. At the news conference were members of the faith community and Frederica Gray, Freddie Gray's twin sister. During that news conference, the Mayor said, "…and we also gave those who wished to destroy space as well." It was a slipup. Anyone who has ever spoken in public has misspoken. It happens to all of us. Your mouth moves just a bit faster than your brain and out comes the wrong thing. She was trying to say we gave people room to protest, and when they started to destroy, we moved in. It was a simple mistake. If you go back and read her remarks in their entirety, or watch the news conference, it's clear what she intended to say. But the media and her political enemies seized on the misstep as proof that she had allowed the violence to take place.

To say that was a disingenuous position would be polite. That narrative, however, had real consequences on how people acted and the morale of the police department. She immediately clarified what she had said, but to no avail. For almost thirty-six subsequent hours, that firestorm raged on social media, in the mainstream media, and in homes across Baltimore. It was a foolish distraction from the real issues she was trying to address. Rather than talk about the fact that she had brought together a coalition representing a broad cross-section of Baltimore, the media was focused on a few words uttered in error.

I am asked about that statement at almost every conference where I present. When I explain the whole situation, the typical response is, "Oh, that makes sense. OK, then." In the heightened emotions of the time, however, seemingly no one was willing to listen. It was in this context that the mayor made the decision to sign the declaration of emergency, and the National Guard began to enter Baltimore. As for the mayor, I sat in briefings with her four or five times a day, every day, from April 27 to May 3.

Often, the meeting was just the commissioner, the mayor, the governor, and a few of us at the staff level. What I saw during those days was a mayor committed to saving her city. She was heavily involved in the daily management of the crisis. She was engaged regarding the issues and the concerns of all sides. She was doing what a leader should do: take in all the information and make reasoned decisions. Frankly, all the experience that she had dealing with natural disasters made her better prepared than just about anyone else in the room. She remained a tireless advocate for the businesses and residents who were impacted by the subsequent curfew and tremendous law enforcement presence in the city. At the same time, she was deeply concerned about the health and safety of all the police officers in Baltimore. She was not a passive viewer of the events of the day. Other people may have handled the situation differently than she did. From my unique perspective, often from behind closed doors, I saw a mayor who never faltered in her desire to do the right thing. I only wish the rest of the city and my department could have seen how hard she worked to bring Baltimore together.

—●—

I have always liked the little things. A flower growing out of a crack in a sidewalk, the colors of the sky at sunset, or fog rolling across a field will stop me in my tracks. It is in these moments that I find my connection to God. Those moments to me are little gifts. They are reminders that beauty is all around us if we only pause for a moment to see it. I've become a collector of the little moments. Every day I try to find three beautiful things to be thankful for. It can be a smile from a stranger, a warm breeze, or a tree blooming on the sidewalk, despite the concrete jungle that I live in. These moments sustain me. It isn't really a surprise to me that my memories of the rest of April 27 are consumed by the little moments.

I feel like I spent the day bouncing from one little moment to the next. There was the conversation with the sergeant who informed me a platoon hadn't had food or water for nearly sixteen hours, and the ensuing search to find a pizza restaurant that would deliver food to them. It was the conversation in the hallway with Detective Dale Wood, telling him to photograph everything, as people were frenetically moving around us talking about the need to memorialize everything for future generations to understand what we were experiencing. It was catching the eye of Lt. Col. Melissa Hyatt to exchange a knowing glance and then stepping into the hallway to talk about what topic I would brief next. It was little interactions with my team, making sure they were OK and had a moment to talk to their families. It was the text message that I sent home telling Jeff to stay in the building, keep the doors locked, and avoid the windows. When I wasn't briefing or talking to reporters on the phone, I spent a lot of time in front of screens. On this large bank of monitors I could see the disorder across the city. Slowly, ever so slowly, we began to gain ground. Somewhere around 2:00 a.m., the city had stabilized. Fires were still burning, and there were still roving bands of looters; the intersection of Pennsylvania and North Avenues, or PennNorth, was still a no-man's land of anarchy. But for the most part, the city had paused.

The watch center is near the top of headquarters in downtown Baltimore. With an all-glass wall facing north, it was easy to see huge sections of the city from west to east. In front of these windows, sometime after things had started to settle, I watched the fires. As far as I could see to my left and then to my right, there were fires. In that moment, history was once again my quiet friend. As I watched buildings burning, I thought about the British bombardment during the War of 1812. I thought of the Pratt Street Riots at the beginning of the Civil War. I envisioned the struggle of the firefighters during the Great Baltimore Fire of

1904. Images from the 1968 riots flashed through my mind. As a city, we had been here before. We would recover. Somehow.

CHAPTER 14

The Waves Keep Crashing

---

*To err is human. To blame someone else
is politics.*

—HUBERT H. HUMPHREY

When I'm teaching, I talk about the interesting phenomenon of the three-day news cycle. It is not a new occurrence. I imagine that somewhere on the streets of Babylon, some editor stood over a stack of papyrus deciding how to tell the story to his readers. What is notable is the expert precision with which today's media uses the three-day cycle to bring crisis news coverage to the average American. It goes a little something like this:

> **Day One** will always be about the incident. Here we will see footage of the crisis unfolding. If it's a terrorist attack, we will see the truck plowing through the crowd, the people falling out of windows, or the explosion at the airport entrance on an endless loop. Experts will walk the viewer through the response and what is happening on the screen. Absent any real information, they will begin to speculate about what is happening. During CNN's coverage of the San Bernardino attack, their law

enforcement expert, Harry Houck actually said on the air, "…look, I'm speculating like the rest of us here." [26]

Day Two will be about the victims and survivors. Somewhere toward the end of day one, moving into day two, we start to learn who was killed and who survived. In the Las Vegas shooting, it was day two that brought us rescue stories and images of those who were tragically killed, interspersed with videos of people in the backs of cars being driven to hospitals. In the Pulse nightclub shooting, it was images of people lined up to give blood, talking about what they had experienced. Day two will also bring the candlelight vigil and seemingly ubiquitous shot of a mother with her arms wrapped around a child.

Day Three is when we look to blame someone. Someone must be responsible for what happened. Very rarely is the person (or persons) who committed the act to blame. Rather, those who should have known or who should have prevented the act from occurring take the hit. It is an interesting comment on how we assign blame that collectively, we would rather blame someone other than the perpetrator for these incidents. Predictably, on day three, the blame often falls on law enforcement. In Orlando came questions about the delay in police engaging the shooter. In Dallas, following the brutal murder of five officers, came questions about the decision to send in a bomb riding on a robot. In the Nice, France truck attack came questions about why police didn't shoot the driver sooner and why there weren't better barriers to stop the truck from coming down the street in the first place. In

---

[26] "CNN's Harry Houck Speculates 'Some Right-Wing Group' Could Be San Bernardino Shooters." NewsBusters. Accessed September 10, 2018. https://www.newsbusters.org/blogs/nb/curtis-houck/2015/12/02/cnns-harry-houck-speculates-some-right-wing-group-could-be-san.

Las Vegas, the police response and the time it took for them to get to the shooter became the issue.

Let's be clear. In Orlando, Omar Mateen walked into a club and killed forty-nine people. In Dallas, Micah Xavier Johnson shot and killed five officers. In Nice, Mohamed Lahouaiej-Bouhlel murdered eighty-seven people. And it was Stephen Paddock who killed fifty-eight people and injured an additional 851 (422 of whom he shot) in Las Vegas. These are the people who are responsible. In all of these cases, and indeed in most crisis situations, there are legitimate and necessary questions about the government response. Sadly, in the current environment, those questions come at the expense of the public having time to digest who is responsible.

The three-day news cycle is effective for news delivery and one that doesn't offer any indication of changing anytime soon. For those in the midst of the crisis, messaging around that cycle becomes of paramount importance. In Baltimore, it was no different.

The morning after the riots, everything had changed. The dam had broken wide open and the race for blame began with renewed vigor. Shortly after the riots, I did an interview with Bill O'Reilly. I knew his reputation as an aggressive interviewer, and I felt well prepared. Still, throughout the interview, I was hammered with questions about how we could have let this happen, why we weren't better prepared, and why we hadn't used more aggressive techniques to stop the looting and destruction. To be fair, these were legitimate questions. What he was lacking was context. In the rush to blame, subtlety is lost. What were we supposed to have been better prepared for? What does a "purge" mean? How does one prepare for an unknown? We sent officers to Mondawmin in advance of the riot. They were kept in vehicles initially to avoid an overt, hostile presence. The entire focus of aggression toward the BPD was centered around overly aggressive police tactics. In fact, for days, we had been receiving positive news reports about how accommodating and respectful of the protestors we had been. Going in with a massive display of force, aggressively engaging a crowd at the outset, would have only exacerbated the situation. And how much more aggressive did he want us to be? We deployed pepper balls, smoke canisters, pepper sprays, and sent in a heavily armored vehicle. What level of force was he looking for? Drilling down into that degree of specificity wasn't something anyone wanted to do. They had seen a riot; someone had to be blamed.

It wasn't just the media, either. Some of the allied agencies who came into assist did more harm than good. A sheriff from Maryland's eastern shore, speaking with the media, said, "I heard it myself over the Baltimore City police radio that I had tethered to my body-armor vest; I heard it repeatedly. 'Stand down, stand down, stand down! Back up, back up, retreat, retreat!' I couldn't believe those words. Those are words I've never heard in my law enforcement vocabulary."[27] This became the rallying cry of those who believed we had allowed the riot to take place. It was simply untrue. In the PERF after-action report, they were very clear about this point: "PERF was told of rumors that officers were ordered by commanders to 'stand down.' However, the issuance of such an order could not be substantiated through PERF interviews with BPD personnel." PERF was given access to recordings of all the radio channels that were used during the riot. BPD also internally reviewed the recordings. There isn't a single instance in which that allegation can be corroborated.

---

[27] "Sheriff: 'I Was Sick To My Stomach' After Being Told To Stand Down." CBS Baltimore. April 30, 2015. Accessed September 02, 2018. http://baltimore.cbslocal.com/2015/04/30/sheriff-michael-lewis-on-the-stand-down-orders-given-to-city-officers/.

There is a human factor in all of this. People were angry and upset. Rightfully so. What was lost in the immediate finger-pointing was a focus on the very issues that had created the situation in the first place. I've already talked at length about preceding causes, and those are the things that we should have been talking about in the immediate aftermath of the riot. Why did it happen in the first place? What were the factors that contributed to so many thousands of people who felt marginalized by the criminal justice system in Baltimore? We had a moment to consider these critical issues and start moving forward with meaningful reform. Sadly, the blame game took the focus away from those issues and gave too many decision-makers an easy out. Blame the training, blame the response, blame the commanders; make those things the issue. There was a legitimate and important need to evaluate the Baltimore Police Department's response to the riots on April 27. Lessons needed to be learned, experiences needed to be memorialized, policies and practices needed to change for the better. All of that is right and good. Still, the response never addressed the fundamental issue that still plagues cities and towns across America today.

Over the course of the next six days, that was the living experience in Baltimore. Every day felt like the movie *Groundhog Day*. Sleep for a few hours, wake up, often in my uniform, do interviews, put out updates, try to manage the narrative, repeat. It was an unending blur of little to no food, lots of caffeine, little to no sleep, lots of talking, little to no time to see the big picture, lots of meetings, little to no time to process what had happened, lots of lurching from one urgent situation to the next.

What never stopped was the meticulous investigation that was taking place. We still needed to find the cause of Freddie Gray's death. That investigation never faltered.

The police commissioner had promised that we would turn over the entirety of the investigation to the state's attorney's office on May 1. Somewhere during the evening of April 29, it became clear that the team had gathered as much information as they could, and it was a tremendous amount. They had laser-mapped the entire route Gray had traveled on foot, reviewed hundreds of hours of video, conducted dozens and dozens of interviews, spoken with experts, and worked with the medical examiner's office to understand the mechanism of injury. They had performed detailed blood and DNA analysis, taken hundreds of photographs that had to be reviewed, and so on. This wasn't NCIS; the facts weren't going to come together in a neat forty-five-minute package. These investigations take time. It was a grueling, laborious, nonstop process that was chronicled in great detail by Justin George in his subsequent articles.

With the team reporting that there was no reason to assume any new groundbreaking information would be uncovered, we decided to turn the investigation over a day early. There was no reason to hold on to it for an extra day. If we found something new, it could always be added as an addendum, but the people of Baltimore wanted to know we were serious about the work we were doing as an organization. Early in the morning on April 30, the case was turned over to the state's attorney's office, in person. An hour later, we walked out onto the bricks in front of headquarters and announced to the press that we had turned the case over.

I had spent the early part of the morning getting everything ready for the briefing. By the time I had finished all of my phone calls, put together some quick talking points, and distributed them, I had about fifteen minutes left before the briefing was about to begin. I called over to the state's attorney's office to give them a courtesy call that we were about to make the announcement.

I should have called them earlier, but I was caught up in the mechanics of putting together a news conference. The news that we were about to hold the briefing was met with incredulity by the person I was speaking with, and the person hung up on me. It was not a surprise when, the next day, as the office announced charges against six of our officers, they called us fifteen minutes in advance to let us know what they were about to do. Politics, sadly, are real.

On May 3, the state of emergency ended in the city. The National Guard and allied agencies left the city. Businesses reopened, the curfew was lifted, and people started to figure out what this new reality meant for the city. For those who had come to assist, they could now return to their normal lives. For the rest of us, the future was fraught with the possibility that this could happen again in a split second. We would never be the same after what had happened. The financial toll was easy to calculate: millions of dollars in damage and tens of millions in associated police costs. The emotional and psychical costs, however, would be far harder to calculate and take much longer to assess.

CHAPTER 15

Time to Leave

Lord help my poor soul.

—EDGAR ALLEN POE

I went to Space Camp when I was ten. It was as cool as it sounds. Well, if you're a science geek like I am, then it was as cool as it sounds. For a week I was exposed to the greatness of NASA, and it was an experience that has stayed with me since. As I grew older, my love of space morphed into a love of sci-fi. *Star Trek*, *Star Wars*, *Battlestar Galactica*—all served as fuel for my inner nerd. On a clear night, I can lose hours staring at stars. I need Virgin or SpaceX to hurry up: I want to go into space before I die. I want to see the universe with my own eyes. For me, the mysteries of the universe are the perfect blend of science and religion. Who are we? Where did we come from? What is the role of God in all this? All those answers are in space as far as I'm concerned. I'm fascinated by the idea that all our atoms are made of exploded stars. We are truly of the universe. I want to know more.

In those first days of Space Camp, I was taught about Newton's laws of motion. The second law, having to do with velocity, has very little meaning to me. The first and the third, however, if ever there were lessons for life, they are contained therein. The first is simple: An object at rest stays at rest until something exerts force upon it, or it stays in motion until something stops it. The third: There is an equal and opposite reaction for every action. Of course, the laws are much more mathematical in their language. I've boiled them down. The lessons, though, are complex and powerful. In life, people will stay still or keep moving unless something acts on them. For every step or action they take, there will be consequences. So simple and yet so profound.

The Baltimore Police Department (and to a large extent the law enforcement profession) has been both stationary and constantly moving. Deeply resistant to change, the department and profession are both constantly engaged in change and action. Every day, police officers interact with communities. Technology is constantly evolving and adapting. Yet, the core way in which law enforcement does its job remains unchanged. Respond to the call, see the crime, take enforcement action, repeat. I'll talk more about this later. For now, it's the third law that I want to talk about. For every action, there is an equal and opposite reaction. Our actions have consequences. The decisions we collectively made as an organization for decades, and in the moments of the riot, had real consequences for the lives of the people we touched. And now we had to live with those consequences. They, in turn, would have an impact on how the agency and the city moved forward.

On July 8, 2015, we hosted the first after-action session facilitated by the Police Executive Research Forum. In a downtown Hilton conference room, we all gathered around tables shaped into a giant U. I had spent the better part of the preceding month gathering reports, personal assessments, witness statements, and public reports about the riot and the days leading up to it. It took me weeks to get it all together and put it into an eighty-five-page report titled *2015 Baltimore Civil Unrest—Looking Back, Moving Forward.* It was a raw, completely uncensored, internal look at what happened. We didn't edit anyone's accounts. If they wrote it, it went into the report. That report was given to PERF in advance of the session and was the document from which they would be conducting their assessment. We invited representatives of every agency that had assisted during the riot to add their unedited accounts to the process. We were committed to transparency and finding ways to move forward.

That morning, the Fraternal Order of Police, Lodge Number 3 released their own after-action report. The timing was not coincidental. Filled with unsubstantiated claims, falsehoods, and propaganda, it spread like wildfire throughout the offices of the city's elected officials and the homes and workplaces of the city's residents. The mayor's office released a statement, saying:

> It is disappointing that the FOP continues to issue baseless and false information instead of working with us to find solutions that will protect our officers. The FOP is using the same sad playbook they relied on when they opposed our efforts to reform state laws and hold officers who act out of line accountable for their actions.
>
> Our hope was that this report would shed some additional light on how we can better prepare our officers should there be future unrest. Instead, this report is no more than a trumped up political document full of baseless accusations, finger pointing and this is not a time for finger pointing and politics. The public and our officers need solutions based on all of the facts. The FOP declined to wait and gather all of the information before rushing to conclusions which is a disservice to our officers who acted so courageously during the unrest.

We will not follow the same approach. Unlike the
FOP, our reviews will offer the citizens and officers
more than a rehash of tired political rhetoric. Our
review will be extensive, independent and consist
of all of the facts.

The statement was a brutal repudiation of the document. It did
little, however, to quell the growing furor. The homicide rate
was starting to spike in the wake of the riots, officer morale was
at an all-time low, and the political friends of several members
of the command staff were lobbying hard for Commissioner
Batts to be fired and replaced with their chosen successor.

The report was released just as our review session got underway.
I spent half the time reading the FOP's report and half the time
listening to what was being said. It was a distraction we didn't
need from the day's events. Shortly after lunch, Commissioner
Batts pulled me out into the hallway. The session was in full
swing, with tempers flaring and accusations being leveled across
the table. I didn't want to be pulled out. I wanted to be in the
room to hear what was being said. I was worried how it would
be spun afterward, and I wanted to have a full accounting of
everything that was said.

In the hallway, the Commissioner looked me in the eyes and
said, "I have to go to City Hall. They're going to take my badge.
It's over." I didn't know what to do or what to say. I was stunned.
All the sound in the hallway faded into the distance. I could
feel my heart racing and my head was swimming in confusion.
This was about more than just the man. This was everything
he represented. This was the end of our push to transition into
a guardian relationship with our community. It was the end of
trying to treat the disease and not the symptom. It was the end of
our hopes and dreams for a new way of policing.

He didn't wait for me to respond. It was a merciful act of kindness. The man who had been a mentor to me for two-and-a-half years knew enough to know I needed time to digest what was happening.

I found myself walking down the hall into an empty conference room. Both Chief of Staff Ganesha Martin and Lt. Col. Melissa Hyatt tried to come in and talk to me; I still had a job to do. This time, I wasn't having it. I brushed them both off and stared out the window at Camden Yards. The one part of my rational brain that was still functioning noted with some degree of irony that it was there in front of Camden Yards that the beginning of the end had started with the violence on April 24. I don't know how long I stayed in the room. I do know that the session had come to an end. All of the reporters had gone to City Hall for the announcement. I had a brief phone call with the new interim police commissioner to review his talking points, and then I drove myself back to headquarters in silence.

I sat in my office for an hour with the door closed. I needed to figure out what to do. After some reflection, I went up to see Interim Commissioner Kevin Davis. There, I offered him my resignation. It was the only proper thing to do. I had been the public face of not just the riots but of the Batts administration. I was inexorably linked with him and his agenda. If the new commissioner had any chance of succeeding, he had to do it with a different face leading the charge. He refused my resignation and instead told me he was promoting me to be his new chief of staff. I thanked him for the offer and asked if I could think about it for a day or two. Not that I really had a choice; when the commissioner tells you that you are doing something, you're doing it. I needed to think, and I needed time. He was kind enough to say yes.

I wasn't sure what I wanted to do. I loved being a cop. I loved my department, and the chance to be chief of staff would be an incredible career boost. It would put me on the fast track to becoming a deputy commissioner and possibly leading my own department one day. It would also put me in a position to closely shape the next administration's strategy for the department. At the same time, the demons I had been wrestling with about the role of law enforcement and its impact on society were real. Every day I was reminded that the very way we were operating was doing real harm to communities. It was not out of malice; we just hadn't found a better way. The cycle of mass incarcerations was continuing, and the solutions I had just spent almost three years of my life working on were now gone in an instant.

The idea of leaving a police department before retirement is anathema to the rank and file. You do your time so you can retire with your pension. Your pension looms over everything you do. Daily conversations are peppered with comments like "only five years to go," or the even more telling, "I did my twenty; I can walk at any time." Practically, it makes sense. You work hard, you get to retire with your pension. From a moral standpoint, though, it always irked me. I always felt that the pension shouldn't be the driving motivator. We're talking about a profession in which every day brings the risk of death or serious injury. It's a profession that has unimaginable consequences, both good and bad, on the people with whom we interact. To simply show up with the goal of getting one day closer to retirement doesn't reflect the sacred oath we all took. I always said the day I stopped wanting to come to work was the day I would find something else to do. The consequences for me and for the community I served were too real.

On the heels of what we had just endured, it would be easy to understand why anyone would leave the department. Many did. For me, it wasn't the experience of the riot; it was what it represented that was clawing at me. My whole life has been about trying to help people. Was I really helping people in the best way by staying? Could I do more in a different role? Two things happened within hours of each other that answered that question for me.

Sitting at my desk, I received a phone call from Judy Pal. Having left the BPD more than a year earlier, she was now serving as the director of operations for FBI-LEEDA, a nonprofit organization that had built itself out of alumni of the FBI National Academy. The National Academy is like boot camp for police executives. It's a multiweek, high-intensity training program designed to prepare police executives for leadership. It is an incredible honor to attend the academy, and the training is top notch. FBI-LEEDA was created to bring that same level of training to police departments across the country. Many agencies couldn't afford to send officers to the National Academy, so this was a way to bring the training to them. She offered me an instructor position with the organization. It was an incredible opportunity that spoke to the core of what I wanted to do. Here was an opportunity to exert a huge influence on police departments across the country. I was very intrigued, but not fully sold on the idea.

As it turns out, my decision about staying or leaving was made for me shortly after the phone call with Judy. Following Kevin Davis's appointment as interim commissioner, he and several senior commanders held a meeting in the headquarters building for all the plain-clothes units, just like the one I used to be in. Meeting in the fifth-floor auditorium, the purpose was to reenergize the officers to go out and work hard to tackle skyrocketing homicide numbers. When you're in front of a group, it's not easy to remember everything that's said, so it's important to have someone taking notes you can review later.

Typically, at meetings like this, I would stand in the back taking those notes. The auditorium gave me the unique opportunity to stand at the rear of the stage, out of sight.

Generation after generation of officers have had their academy graduation and promotional ceremonies in this room that holds 500, with its wooden seats reminiscent of every high school auditorium designed in the 1950s or 60s. The towering ceiling was supported by walls illuminated with impressive sconce lighting. It was both a majestic and outdated space. Every time I walked into the room, I would think of the four times I had walked across the stage. It was always in my Class-A dress uniform with white gloves. Swelling patriotic music would fill the space. The National Anthem would be sung and the Pledge of Allegiance recited. It was a place of dignity and ceremony. Usually, the room was packed with proud family and friends. I was used to this room being a place of celebration and tradition.

Today was different. There was a dark and somber feeling in the room. No one knew what to expect. Seats creaked and groaned as restless officers tried to get comfortable. There isn't a seat that has been invented that you can sit in comfortably wearing a gun belt and ballistic vest. As the meeting began, I found myself on the stage, behind the curtains. It was a great place to stand, as I could clearly hear all the questions being asked without being a visible presence. The message being delivered was a simple one: The riot was over. We were back to basics. Do whatever it took to get the homicide number down. After all, it was what we knew how to do. Then I heard it—the moment that made my decision for me. I heard one of the deputy police commissioners say, "The days of Batts are over. It's time to go out there and do what you know how to do." For the second time in as many days, I felt my world come to a crushing stop.

Any hope I had of continuing to move forward with our efforts to reform the organization died in that moment. Here was one of the most senior people in the organization telling plain-clothes officers to go out and do whatever it took to reduce crime. Whatever it took. That mentality and operating modality were the *exact reasons* we had just gone through a riot, the reasons people had protested the department for weeks on end, the reasons nearly 200 officers were injured, millions of dollars in property had been destroyed, and lives irrevocably changed. No lessons had been learned. Nothing was different. How could I, knowing what I knew, seeing what I had seen, continue to represent an organization that was intentionally reverting to what it had been?

I didn't wait for the meeting to end. I left the auditorium and started walking back to my office. As I crossed the catwalk in the atrium, I looked out the giant windows at Fayette Street and I-83. Just two short months before, National Guard Humvees with soldiers carrying automatic weapons had been in the exact spot at which I was looking. I made my decision. It was time to go.

———•———

Friday afternoon, I told a few people that I was going to take the weekend to think about it, but I was likely going to resign on Monday. To varying degrees, each of them tried to get me to think carefully about what I was considering. Some didn't want to see me throw away a promising future. Others didn't want to lose my companionship in the department. I listened to all of them, but my heart wasn't in it. I was already saying goodbye. That weekend was a horrendous conflict of emotions. I spent most of it with Jeff, walking around the neighborhood or sitting on the couch and talking about what our future would look like. It was uncertain, and I was as terrified about what I was about to do as I was sure that I had to do it. I was thirty-seven years old. Almost my entire adult life had been spent with the BPD. It wasn't just what I knew—it was who I was. Yet I felt compelled by my own moral compass. I would move forward and try to do what I could to bring necessary change to the profession.

I didn't sleep Sunday night. When the alarm went off Monday morning, I suddenly felt like a weight had been lifted from my shoulders. I felt the tension and panic shifting to determination to embark upon this next part of my life with an open mind and willing heart. I ran into Ganesha Martin, my division chief, and Melissa Hyatt in the garage as I was parking my car. I had talked with both on Friday, and they wanted to know my decision. I told them I was on my way up to see the interim commissioner and tell him Friday would be my last day. They both lowered their heads in what seemed like quiet resignation. I walked into the building, got on the elevator that was so familiar to me, and went up to a commissioner's office which now seemed so foreign to me.

In this office, I had worked through critical incidents with Commissioner Batts. With its commanding view of President Street and Fayette Street as a background, we had tackled officer misconduct, waxing and waning crime statistics, personnel changes, and myriad other issues. We also had long talks about philosophy, religion, politics, history, science, and the ever-present desire to end disparate treatment of minorities. We had staged media interviews in this room and celebrated birthdays and retirements. And it was in this room where I told Davis that I was leaving the department. He said he understood and shook my hand. The next day, the *Baltimore Sun* put out an article about my departure which he retweeted, saying I was one of the best. On Wednesday, he accused me of trying to sabotage him with a media interview that I knew nothing about and stopped talking to me. It was an inauspicious way to end my career.

I left the building Friday afternoon with no fanfare. I took one last look at my briefing room, taking a photo of the podium I had spent countless hours at, and I walked out the door for the last time.

My worst fears about the order to go out and do whatever it took came to life in 2017, when the U.S. attorney's office indicted the entire Gun Trace Task Force Unit. The corruption and abuse of power was staggering to read.[28] It seemed like a script for the next *Training Day* movie. Starting in 2015, and ramping up in 2016, the forty-five-page indictment laid out a conspiracy by the sergeant and six detectives to defraud the city, rob people on the streets of Baltimore, and frame innocent people for crimes they had never committed. They wrote false search and seizure warrants to steal from houses, submitted thousands of dollars in false overtime slips, and drove around with pellet guns in their glove compartments to plant on someone if they shot them. It outlined a level of corruption that is as boggling and disgusting to me as it is telling—all of it committed while the department was actively under a civil rights investigation.

I'm not saying the order given in the auditorium led to these criminal acts, but it certainly set the stage for them. The unit was, during the time of their crime spree, getting illegal guns off the street. They were targeting known gun offenders and arresting them. To anyone in the upper echelon looking at the unit, they were a high-speed, high-performance team doing exactly what they needed them to do. The message was clear: so long as you perform, no one is going to look too closely. Go out and do what needs to be done and we will leave you alone.

---

[28] "Document: Indictment against Seven Baltimore Police Officers." Baltimoresun.com. March 01, 2017. Accessed September 10, 2018. http://www.baltimoresun.com/news/maryland/crime/bal-document-indictment-against-seven-baltimore-police-officers-20170301-htmlstory.html.

It is incomprehensible to me that members were able to submit overtime reports without supervisors being aware that they were out of state. I was a supervisor from 2007-2015, and for each and every unit I supervised, I knew where my people were. I knew what they were doing and when they were working. I certainly knew if they were on vacation in another state. That an entire unit was able to act as a criminal enterprise means that they weren't being supervised. They weren't being supervised because they were putting numbers on the board, all to get the homicide number down. After all, that's really all that mattered.

CHAPTER 16

Crushing Darkness

Today my forest is dark. The trees are sad and all the butterflies have broken wings.

—RAINE COOPER

T o feel lost in oneself is perhaps the most terrible experience of all. All the lights are dimmer than they should be, the struggle to breathe is harder than it must be, and time is an enemy that marks each second of pain in its endless, relentless march. There is no joy, there is no release; there is only the quiet feeling of falling deeper into a chasm that has no bottom. To be sad is to know that there will come a time when you aren't sad. To feel lost, to be engulfed in the great gulf of depression, is to know it will never end. That is where I found myself by December 2015.

It wasn't just the mental toll. There was a physical price as well. On May 5, two days after the state of emergency was lifted, I ended up in the emergency room. Driving to work, I felt a pain rip through my body. It was like nothing I had ever experienced before. I had to pull my car over to the side of the road, and I ended up being transported to the hospital. Stress can do incredible things to the human body. In my case, I ended up with severe intestinal issues. Months of treatment, testing, and giant horse pills followed. I will live with those ramifications for the rest of my life.

The downward spiral was longer in coming; it didn't happen all at once. Rather, it was a slow, unstoppable, unavoidable slide. I was trapped on an escalator that had no end in sight and no way for me to stop it. There were days when I found it impossible to get out of bed. The very effort to use the bathroom consumed all the energy that I had. No one and nothing brought me joy. Sleep was an elusive escape, and I was oh so tired. Yet I would close my eyes and the images and sounds would come: "We're getting fucking slaughtered!" "Signal 13, we have an officer down!" "We need help, now!" There was the flash of the TV screen, rocks hurled from atop a hill at a line of blue. Next came the aerial shot of surging crowds and officers holding the line. Images of reporters lined up waiting to ask me question after question about what we did wrong.

Then would come flashbacks of conversations that I would play out in my head over and over. Critical moments were rehashed as my brain desperately sought a new solution to what was inevitable. Day after day, night after night, the bad movie never stopped. It was a constant loop that played in my mind. Even today, as I write this, I can still hear the screams on the radio. The only thing I could think to tell people was that I was tired. I didn't know how else to describe what I was feeling, what was happening to me. I love words; I relish the ability to convey thought and action through them. Yet, I couldn't find any. "I'm tired," was the best I could muster. It was lonely and terrifying, and I wanted it all to end. I just wanted to end. Maybe then the screams would stop.

As each day passed, I couldn't shake the feeling that I was responsible for what had happened. It was my job to make sure that we were properly communicating our message. That we showed the people of Baltimore, the world, who we truly were and what we were about. That we did understand the concern and frustration—not just at an intellectual level, that we felt the same sense of angst and despair. That we, too, wanted to change the department for the better. It was my job to make sure everyone understood that to be true. To me, if I had done my job the right way, I could have stopped the onslaught headed our way. If I had spoken just enough of the right words, I would have protected my department, I would have protected my city, and I would have kept each of our 3,000 officers safe. That was my responsibility. In the months after I left the department, more and more, the feeling of failure consumed me.

I had not done the very thing I was charged with. We had a riot. Officers were badly injured. I carried each of their injuries and their families' fears in my soul. I was gutted by the knowledge that the good people of Baltimore couldn't trust their police because I hadn't convinced them.

It must seem strange to think that I would shoulder all that responsibility. I'm not a martyr. Nor do I want sympathy. However, in those dark, endless days, no one could tell me otherwise.

Something needed to change. I couldn't go on like that. My wonderful husband supported me in every way he could and was able to convince me to go get help. I resisted at first. I didn't want help. I deserved the pain I was in. It was my due.

The process of getting help was not easy. Doctors put me on powerful anti-depressants for post-traumatic stress disorder (PTSD). I couldn't understand why they were telling me it was PTSD. In my career, I had been shot at more times than I cared to remember, had been in brutal fights, had a serious car accident, and had seen enough homicides and shootings to last a lifetime.

Yet, none of it really bothered me. I was able to cope and deal with those things. I had good outlets. I was able to understand each of those events in their context. PTSD was for soldiers or the incredibly brave officers who stood on the front lines and endured brutal assaults. It was for those who had been exposed to far worse events than I ever was. The diagnosis enraged me. I didn't warrant that kind of diagnosis. It wasn't fair to all those who had *real* PTSD.

Then my therapist said something brilliantly insightful to me. "You were prepared for those things; you trained for them. You expected them. How could you prepare or train for what you just went through?" What took place in Baltimore was far out of the ordinary. It was extraordinary. He went on to explain that, to him, it was clear that as one of the senior people in a decision-making role, with the responsibilities I was entrusted with, I was carrying the burden of the entire event on my shoulders. I felt responsible for everything that had happened, and that in and of itself was traumatic. To be exposed to that level of trauma, for the number of days that I was exposed to it, does severe and lasting damage. It was like a lightbulb went off in my head. Suddenly, it all made sense. For the first time in months, the downward descent stopped.

None of this is easy to talk about. It's like ripping an adhesive bandage from a fresh wound. There are times when the memories are as real to me today as they were the day they happened. I have better ways of dealing with them now. They are not the all-consuming nightmare they used to be. Still, in the moment, these memories can be powerful and emotional. It's not easy to talk about; it is also incredibly important to talk about. Mental health in law enforcement is the great taboo. To expose a mental health issue is to expose the greatest of all weaknesses. In the law enforcement culture, you don't get to have emotions; they make you weak. Weakness is to be avoided at all costs. If you're weak, it will be worn like a scarlet letter for the rest of your career. You had just better suck it up like everyone else.

Beyond the cultural ramifications, getting mental health assistance can be detrimental to an officer's career. Any officer who admits to needed help will likely have his or her badge and gun taken the instant those words are uttered. There is liability to consider. An agency can't in good conscience allow someone with mental health issues to be wandering the streets with a loaded gun. That suspension can impact promotions, transfers, overtime pay—the list goes on. So, you don't get help. Even anonymous counseling has its issues. Cops don't trust people to start with. Spend each day having people lie to you; you would start to doubt everyone as well. So of course, if you go get help anonymously, the department *will* find out, and you *will* end up dealing with the same consequences as if you had told someone anyway. The system itself makes it very difficult to get help.

There are real-world consequences for this Catch-22. An estimated 140-150 officers take their own lives each year.[29] That's twelve human beings who will end their own lives each month. That means twelve families a month will lose a husband, wife, father, mother, sister, brother, son or daughter. Suicide kills more police officers each year than anything else. Yet it is seen as weakness. I assisted one department in planning a funeral for an officer who had committed suicide. There was pushback from some members of leadership in that organization about participating in the funeral because the officer was "too weak to deserve a funeral." That mentality is pervasive and disgusting, especially when the numbers show this is a much larger issue for law enforcement than is acknowledged.

---

[29] O'Hara, Andy. "It's Time We Talk About Police Suicide." The Marshall Project. June 04, 2018. Accessed September 02, 2018. https://www.themarshallproject.org/2017/10/03/it-s-time-we-talk-about-police-suicide.

A 2008 study found 31.9 percent of officers surveyed screened positive for PTSD.[30] That's nearly one out of every three police officers. Most police stress is cumulative in nature, as incident after incident builds on existing trauma. Another study found those with multiple PTSD incidents have an even higher risk of morbidity and dysfunction.[31] Suicide isn't the only risk. The Hazelden Betty Ford Foundation found that 37.6 percent of officers exhibited one or more problem drinking behaviors.[32] The research shows that officers have a much higher percentage rates of depression, PTSD, burnout, and other anxiety-related mental health conditions.[33]

I don't think I'm a weak person. I've been an openly gay man my entire adult life. I've endured more crap than most people should ever have to go through. I've been taunted, spit on, assaulted, berated by colleagues, denied backup, and refused service in restaurants. I spent more than a decade working on the streets of one of the most violent cities in America. I push myself to be a better person today than I was the day before. I don't consider myself weak in the slightest. Still, I am a person who fights with depression and PTSD daily. We all have burdens that we carry. No one knows someone else's struggles, and to create a culture that punishes those who want to get help and better themselves is toxic.

---

[30] Asmundson, Gordon J. G., and Jennifer A. Stapleton. "Associations Between Dimensions of Anxiety Sensitivity and PTSD Symptom Clusters in Active-Duty Police Officers." *Cognitive Behaviour Therapy* 37, no. 2 (2008): 66-75. doi:10.1080/16506070801969005.

[31] Karam, Elie G., Matthew J. Friedman, Eric D. Hill, Ronald C. Kessler, Katie A. Mclaughlin, Maria Petukhova, Laura Sampson, Victoria Shahly, Matthias C. Angermeyer, Evelyn J. Bromet, Giovanni De Girolamo, Ron De Graaf, Koen Demyttenaere, Finola Ferry, Silvia E. Florescu, Josep Maria Haro, Yanling He, Aimee N. Karam, Norito Kawakami, Viviane Kovess-Masfety, María Elena Medina-Mora, Mark A. Oakley Browne, José A. Posada-Villa, Arieh Y. Shalev, Dan J. Stein, Maria Carmen Viana, Zahari Zarkov, and Karestan C. Koenen. "Cumulative Traumas And Risk Thresholds: 12-Month Ptsd In The World Mental Health (Wmh) Surveys." *Depression and Anxiety* 31, no. 2 (2013): 130-42. doi:10.1002/da.22169.

[32] Butler Center for Research. "Alcohol Abuse Among Police Officers." Jellinek Curve of Addiction | Hazelden Betty Ford Foundation. Accessed September 02, 2018. https://www. hazeldenbettyford.org/education/bcr/addiction-research/alcohol-abuse-police-ru-716.

[33] "NAMI." National Alliance on Mental Illness. Accessed September 02, 2018. http://www. nami.org/Find-Support/Law-Enforcement-Officers.

Any meaningful reform in law enforcement must start with an understanding of the mental health challenges faced by police officers across the country. That means we must remove the taboo and stigma associated with mental health treatment. Again, it's about treating the disease, not the symptoms. Departments must invest in the mental health of their officers. That means making mental health screenings as mandatory as firearms requalification or in-service training. The only way to remove stigma is to make sure everyone is doing the same thing. I can already hear chiefs and town managers screaming about the cost. That is a very superficial view. What are the secondary and tertiary costs of officers in mental health crises? How do their behaviors manifest in daily interactions with citizens, in disciplinary issues, or in medical leave? There is also, and more importantly, a moral side to this issue. We expect and demand police officers to go out and protect our communities. Why aren't we in turn doing everything we can to protect them?

Communities need healthy cops on the street. Think about all the public and private services that you use. Which of those services would you be OK with receiving from an intoxicated provider? Do you want an officer struggling with undiagnosed and untreated depression, anxiety, or PTSD making split-second decisions in a deadly-force encounter? Do you want an officer in such a condition deciding to arrest you or a family member?

We entrust police officers with incredible power. We give them the authority to take people's freedom or their lives. It is incumbent on police departments to better care for their officers and for citizens to demand it.

CHAPTER 17

Taking Stock of the Present

Some men see things as they are, and ask why.

I dream of things that never were, and ask why not.

—Senator Robert Kennedy

loved being a patrol sergeant. I was privileged to work in a number of areas during my career, and I got to see a lot of amazing things. Nothing compared to being a patrol sergeant. It was hard work, managing sixteen different personalities, trying to keep my little sector of the Southern District safe on the midnight shift. I learned a lot about myself, I made a lot of mistakes, and I started to learn how to be an effective leader. Like anything else that is new, there are things I wish I could do differently now. Life is like that; learn from the mistakes and do better next time. I know I did OK in the end, though. All these years later, I'm still friends with a few of the officers who worked in that squad.

Like any supervisor, you start to develop little pet peeves. The thing that would make me bonkers would be when an officer came up to me and said, "Sarge, I can't find the keys to my patrol car." It would happen during shift change; the Charlie shift was coming off the street and the Adam shift was getting ready to go out. By tradition, the relieving officer is supposed to meet the outgoing officer at their car. That way they can exchange important information and hand over the equipment, like keys. That was how it was supposed to work, and for the most part, it did. For any number of reasons, however, that didn't always happen. Enter the dreaded "I can't find the keys to my patrol car." I'm reasonably certain I started to develop a Pavlovian left-eye twitch reaction to that statement.

My response would be a simple one—an answer that anyone might give: "Did you look?" In other words, did you check the car, not just the ignition? Did you check the Charlie shift office? Did you look in the locker room for the officer? Have you asked anyone else if they might have knowledge of the present location of the aforementioned keys?

Just as predictable as my question was the response. "Yep, I checked the car, they aren't there." *Insert facepalm here.* I wanted my officer out on the street. If I just found the keys, then they could go out and be productive. So, like Javert in *Les Miserables*, I would begin my quest for the bread thief...I mean keys. It took me some time to learn to stop looking for them myself.

And as a great homage to the grizzled police sergeants who had come before me, I mastered the art of the expressionless face. "Sarge, I can't find my keys." *Blink...Blink...*

It was this learning process that taught me one of the most valuable lessons of my career. I never went to someone with just a problem. I would always bring a solution as well. It might not be the solution they wanted to see or hear, but I made the effort. I went beyond just identifying the issue. I also tried to find a means of solving it.

That is exactly what I have spent the last three years of my life trying to do. Find a solution to one of the biggest problems facing America today: the relationships between police and communities. In both my role as a professional consultant and as an instructor with FBI-LEEDA, I have had the opportunity to travel to more than sixty cities in forty states across the country. I've trained more than 1,600 police officers and met with hundreds more. I've had the chance to talk to business owners, elected officials, residents, students, and more than a few airline employees. I've learned a tremendous amount about the national mood regarding police and what police think in return. This broad spectrum of sentiment has given me a unique perspective about the challenges that we need to collectively overcome in order to start to heal the growing rift between communities, especially minority communities, and the police officers who work tirelessly to protect them. Coupled with my own history as a police officer in Baltimore and the riots, I want to share what I have seen and what I have learned.

It's far too easy to point out failings. It requires little effort, little thought, and very little skin in the game to point out what someone or some organization is doing wrong. It takes a lot more investment to try and find solutions to problems. This is one of the biggest issues facing law enforcement reform today. It is easy for the critic to sit back and say, "The cops shouldn't have done that; they need more training; that was just wrong."

What does any of that mean? If the cops shouldn't have done something, what should they have done instead? What are you basing that judgment on? What research have you done? What national best practices have you studied? What case law have you researched?

The cops need more training, you say? What kind? Who should do it? What are their qualifications? Why that training over another? How effective is it? Who is going to pay for it?

The cop was just wrong, you tell me. How? Was he wrong ethically, morally, legally? Did he violate a policy that he was trained in, or do you just not like how the outcome looks?

Don't tell me what you think; tell me what you know. I see pundits on television and read editorials in which the provider of opinion is only too happy to pontificate about all the things that went wrong. When they are asked what needs to change, they provide the standard, superficial answer: more training. For a profession that feels constantly under siege, these banal replies do nothing but reinforce the narrative that the public doesn't know what they are talking about.

The most frustrating thing about this never-ending process is that it does nothing—nothing—to address the actual issues that led to (*insert controversy here*) occurring in the first place. If we are truly going to work to change the way police departments engage with communities, then we must go beyond the superficial and address some of the core issues that create animosity, division, misunderstanding, and in some cases deadly uses of force that could have and should have been avoided.

To do that, we have to start from a neutral place. That means police officers must acknowledge that a lawful action doesn't always mean the action was the right thing to do. Justifying an action within policy or within legal merit doesn't take into account the emotional response to that incident. Sometimes there is actually a better way. Starting from a neutral place means departments must understand that it is possible to support law enforcement and still want to see agencies do a better job in the communities where they work. It also means departments need to start holding officers who commit malicious acts publicly accountable, and as quickly as possible. That might mean changing some state laws and labor contracts. It is not an option to continue to operate under the current paradigm. How can any police department expect to have the public trust when they keep their disciplinary system a closely guarded secret?

The public has a role to play in this as well. Finding that neutral ground means that communities need to understand that some people are bad actors. They commit horrendous acts of violence, they destroy communities, and they have no regard for the value of human life. Police officers are the only ones who stand between those people and your families. Communities need to understand that not everyone wants to go to jail willingly. People will fight, and in a fight, you must sometimes use force. That means there are times you're going to have to punch someone, or hit them with a baton, or taser them, or pepper spray them. There is no way to make that look good on video. Let me put it another way. Anyone who has ever tried to put a five-year-old in bed knows what a horrendous struggle that can be if the child does not want to do it. Now, take that same mentality and replace bed with jail and the five-year-old with an adult. See how easy it is now?

When any person or group of people entrench themselves in a mantle of certainty, it leaves very little room for conversations or options. We can all agree that the current trend cannot continue. Communities of color across the country feel as if they are under attack from police officers. Police officers feel marginalized, misunderstood, resented, and underappreciated. If this current cycle of incident, followed by outrage, followed by protests, followed by further entrenchment of both sides continues, the only thing that will happen is an increasing level of frustration and animosity on both sides. The result of that cycle was on full display in Baltimore.

In the immediate future, there is a pressing need for law enforcement agencies to get out into the community and start having real conversations. Police chiefs boast to me all the time about all of the events that they host. We have town hall meetings, citizen police academies, and neighborhood association meetings, they tell me. All of those are good programs and should continue. These programs give departments an opportunity to start providing sorely needed information on how and why police officers do what they do. They offer a safe space for challenging questions to be asked and answered. These types of events also offer an opportunity for community members to share frustrations or praise. But they all require the community to come to the department. They are a passive response to an active problem. I've been to community meetings in police departments all over the country. If you can get 100 people into a room, that is a blockbuster meeting. Even in a small town of 5,000 people, that's barely scratching the surface of all of the people who live and work in the town.

Connecting on social media is a fantastic way to connect with large numbers of people. It doesn't reach enough people, though. Large segments of the community may not use social media, especially when we start talking about the elderly population. The same goes for sending out emails and newsletters. Again, not everyone is going to receive or read them. That's not to say that any of these are bad ideas. In fact, quite the opposite is true. Any opportunity to connect with someone is a good opportunity, and all of the various methods that exist to connect should be embraced. At the end of the day, though, the first thing we need to do is get back to basics.

Police departments need to start sending officers into businesses, churches, community centers, and any other place where officers can connect person to person. A number of agencies do this; however, it's often the community service officer that they send in. While it is helpful in establishing a relationship of sorts, it doesn't give the officer patrolling the neighborhood the chance to make the connections with the people that they are serving. This does a disservice to the community, which doesn't get to know their police, and to the officer, who doesn't get to meet people in a different setting than a call for service. Taking thirty minutes out of every patrol shift just to get out of the car and talk to people has huge benefits. The numbers add up pretty quickly. Talk to five or ten people in that thirty-minute window; multiply that by the number of officers working each shift. Now do that every day. Pretty soon, you're connecting with a whole lot of people in your neighborhood face to face, daily. The more we get to know each other, the more each one in each group starts to see the other as a person, the better the communication becomes.

That's the quick, down and dirty, short-term need that has to be filled. It doesn't, however, address the root cause. For that, we have to have a much more in-depth and substantial conversation about what the expectation is for police officers in a community. There is the often-quoted saying, "Doing the same thing over and over again expecting a different result is the definition of insanity." I would submit that is what law enforcement has been doing for decades. Generations of police officers have gone out, seen a crime, investigated a crime, made an arrest for the crime, and repeated. Crime rates are falling; that is true. Yet media stories are filled with examples of people who have been arrested ten, twenty, thirty times, often for the same crime. That is a system that has failed. This is where people jump in and say that it's the court's fault for letting people off too easily, or the jails' fault for letting them out too soon. *We need tougher judges and tougher sentencing!*

The facts belie that argument. The United States incarcerates 693 people for every 100,000 residents. That number is five times higher than most other nations in the world.[34] When you look into the numbers, it gets even more disturbing. Thirty-three states in the United States have higher incarceration rates in their own right than the next-highest country, which is Turkmenistan.[35] Yet when you look at our crime rate in comparison to other nations, the numbers are fairly consistent. We just jail a lot more people, for a lot longer, than other nations. Logic forces us to concede that if Americans aren't committing crimes at a vastly disproportionate rate, and we are jailing more people than anyone else, how could it possibly be that the system has failed? Clearly, we have no issue putting people in jail.

There is an argument to be made about what our prison policy looks like in comparison to other nations. Sweden has embarked on what could be considered a revolutionary approach to prison policy. Rather than focus on punishment, the Swedes set out to rehabilitate the incarcerated offender. They view the prison sentence as an opportunity to address the issues that led the person to prison in the first place. Because of their efforts, there has been a 40 percent reduction in their recidivism rates.[36] It's worth a look.

That same concept is what we were beginning to look at in Baltimore before the riots and is something that law enforcement should begin to approach in the United States. It is beyond obvious that the current system just doesn't work. It's time for a change.

---

[34] Wagner, Peter, and Alison Walsh. "States of Incarceration: The Global Context 2016." Mass Incarceration: The Whole Pie 2016 | Prison Policy Initiative. Accessed September 03, 2018. https://www.prisonpolicy.org/global/2016.html.

[35] Ibid.

[36] James, Erwin. "'Prison Is Not for Punishment in Sweden. We Get People into Better Shape' | Erwin James." The Guardian. November 26, 2014. Accessed September 10, 2018. https://www.theguardian.com/society/2014/nov/26/prison-sweden-not-punishment-nils-oberg.

CHAPTER 18

A Different Vision

An absolutely new idea is one of the
rarest things known to man.

—THOMAS MORE

H ave you ever read a book and wondered where it was written? I think about that a lot when I'm reading a book. I wonder if the author was sitting in some well-appointed office, a room of the main house filled with comfortable leather chairs and the obligatory crackling fireplace. I imagine a room that is a sanctuary for creativity. I've been thinking about that a lot these past few months. For the most part, I've been writing at our small high-top kitchen table. A good chunk of this book has been written on the road. Right now, I'm actually sitting in a hotel room in Topeka, Kansas, getting ready to teach for another week. Another group of law enforcement professionals will gather tomorrow to spend a week listening to what I have to say. It's a heady responsibility. I have another four-and-a-half days to try to convince a room full of police that there is a better way—that transparency, engagement, understanding, and an open mind are a necessary first step in doing things a better way.

I love being in the classroom. It is a safe space, away from the eyes of the public, where we can have necessary conversations without fear of judgment. I like to push and challenge preconceived notions and try to get people to think in a new and different way. It's that new and different way that I keep coming back to: in my dreams, in my teaching, and now in my writing. I use this example all the time: If IBM were still pushing and marketing typewriters, they would be out of business. They made phenomenal typewriters. I can still remember the one my mom had in her office with the gigantic red *On* switch, super chunky keys, and the sense that you were really accomplishing something as the spinning wheel of letters slammed into the unsuspecting paper. I can't remember the last time I saw one. IBM adapted to technology changes and shifted its business model as a result. I could list any number of businesses that have done the same thing. Yet, in law enforcement, we are still using the same techniques to address crime that we've used for more than a century. It's a simple formula: see a crime, arrest the offender, write a report, testify in court, repeat. It's a formula that is based on an enforcement approach to the reduction of crime.

I have something entirely different in mind. A problem-solving approach to fighting crime. From the outset, let me say this: there will always be people who are willing to break the law, and there will always be a need to arrest those who break the law. However, when you look at some of the incidents that have drawn national attention, there may have been another, better way to address the issue.

Let's start with Eric Garner. Garner died as the New York Police Department attempted to arrest him on July 17, 2014, for selling loose cigarettes. That means he was taking cigarettes out of a pack and selling them individually. Selling cigarettes without a tax stamp is a criminal violation. Garner had a long history with the NYPD. Prior to his death, he had been arrested more than thirty times.

Let's stop there for a second. That isn't normal. Most people go their entire lives without being arrested. To be arrested thirty times is astonishing, yet disturbingly predictable when it comes to incidents that ultimately result in the use of deadly force.

Most of Garner's arrests were for selling loose cigarettes. To be clear, that is a crime. The question that must be asked, though, is after so many arrests for the same thing, why didn't anyone stop and say, "This isn't working"? Clearly, he was doing this for a reason, likely an economic one. The threat of an arrest most obviously was not a deterrent. Yet, time after time, he was arrested for the same crime. That means police resources were being used repeatedly to arrest, process, report, and testify for the same crime. That means state resources were used for booking, transporting, jailing, and legal proceedings. All of that comes at taxpayer expense. That's the business side.

On the human side, what happens if you keep arresting the same person over and over and over? Resentment. In fact, Garner had filed paperwork in federal court alleging that he was being harassed by the NYPD, a case that was still pending at the time of his death.

Now, enter the arguments from both sides. Law enforcement will say this is simple: He was breaking the law, and you don't get to do that. Activists, friends, and supporters will say, yeah but who was he really hurting? By all accounts, he was a friendly guy, well-liked in the neighborhood. He didn't bother or hurt anyone, so why waste time arresting him repeatedly? Stepping back, one can see ways in which both sides are right, and both sides are wrong.

You don't get to break the law. That's not acceptable. At the same time, at what point do you stop and say, why do we keep arresting this guy? Is it in the best interest of the public to continue to use all these public resources on the same thing, time and again? This is the moment when the enforcement modality of law enforcement falls short. If the goal is to reduce crime, how is that reduction achieved through continual arrest of the same person for the same thing?

NYPD's goal was clear: Stop the criminal act from taking place. As evidenced by the number of arrests prior to the July 17 encounter, that goal was never achieved. The arrest served as a short-term impediment to continued behavior.

That is not unique. Freddie Gray was arrested at least eighteen times before his death in BPD custody. In both of these cases the disturbing similarity is that an increasing number of police encounters ultimately results in an in-custody death.

What if there were a better way?

Another old adage goes, "When you're a hammer, every problem starts to look like a nail." When the only tool you give police to solve issues is to arrest, every problem can (and must) be solved with an arrest. We need to equip officers with another, much more powerful tool—time. Time to talk, time to understand, time to examine, time to help. Police officers are the front line for most of society's ills. They are the touchpoint for those in crisis, those who are distressed, those who are committing repeated criminal acts. If we give them time and resources to start examining what the real, underlying cause is for so many of these repeat arrests, we give them the opportunity to start breaking the cycle.

I've talked with thousands of officers in states across the country about time. The response is universal. Any officer who takes the amount of time necessary to start digging into the root causes of the issues plaguing so many cities is admonished by supervisors and peers alike. The system simply isn't designed for that. The longer an officer takes on a call in their assigned service area, the more calls other officers have to handle in that area. That pulls officers out of other locations to handle the backlog and breeds resentment among coworkers. In short, the system is designed to mitigate issues as quickly as possible, either through resolution or arrest, leaving officers available for the next call. The operating modality becomes the norm for officers. That norm creates habits, and habits become the culture of an agency.

Equally important in this process is the role elected officials and departmental leaders play. In order to afford the officer time to address issues, leaders would have to increase staffing, which impacts budgets. They would have to coordinate with other agencies to assist the officer in solving the problem. For example, if an officer continually responded to the same address for disorderly behavior, and she determined that the root cause of the issue was a mental health issue, she would need support from other city agencies to address the mental health issue. That costs money and requires all of the agencies to be on the same page. That just isn't the case right now.

When I talk to departments about this approach, the initial response is to balk at the idea. I hear "That's not police work, that's social work!" I would submit that it is both. The stated goal of any agency is the reduction of crime. Addressing and fixing the root cause of the issue stops the 911 call for service in the first place. That means a crime didn't take place; that means officers have more time to prevent other crimes. Play this out, and in the short term, it means more resources, more coordination, and more time. In the long term, it means fewer repeat calls for service, more critical issues resolved, more time for officers to start addressing other areas of crime, and maybe, just maybe, a better relationship with a community.

There is an additional benefit to this idea that can't be measured in statistical reports or budget analysis. It is, however, potentially the most beneficial aspect of this idea. Police officers will start to see the community they serve as people, and the people they serve will start to see the officers as caring, compassionate human beings. I know both to be true now. I also know, as has been pointed out numerous times in this book, that both sides are currently entrenched in an ideology that stops connection. If we don't start the process of fixing that now, nothing changes. All the training in the world doesn't stop the systemic approach to crime-fighting that creates situation after situation that leads to a deadly-force incident that only further damages the public trust.

I am not naïve. There will always be people who will break the law; there will always be a need for police officers to intervene. That is human nature. Imagine, though, if just for a moment, that in the first encounter with Eric Garner, things had gone differently. Imagine if instead of an arrest, NYPD had had the time, resources, and ability to investigate the reason Garner was selling loose cigarettes in the first place. Was he jobless? Was he trying to make extra money? Was selling loose cigarettes an indicator of a greater psychological issue? Now envision the world in which NYPD had been able to address both the illegality of his actions *and* to get him the type of support that would have made it unnecessary for him to be out there in the first place. That means he *doesn't* get arrested dozens of additional times. It also means that he doesn't die in NYPD custody. That same lesson can apply to Freddie Gray, and to many other deadly-force incidents that have happened across the country.

It also means that the culture of an organization starts to shift. As officers have more time to address issues, they start to approach all their calls differently. How many times have we seen a shaky cell phone video capture an encounter with police that could have easily been prevented if the officers had just slowed down? I'm not blaming the officers. I'm blaming the system that has created a belief that officers don't have time to slow down.

This isn't my opinion alone. I've lived it and seen it firsthand. I've also worked with hundreds of departments across the country where this is also the truth. If we truly want to see a change in law enforcement for the better, then yes, let us do lots of training. Let us examine policies and procedures. Let us better understand the laws we enforce and the reasons for them. Mostly, though, we need to look at the core manner in which we operate. If we don't fix that, history will only continue to repeat itself. Another shooting will happen, tempers will flare, resentment will build, and another community will find itself at war with its police department.

CHAPTER 19

A New Direction

Everyone wants to be seen. Everyone wants to be heard. Everyone wants to be recognized as the person that they are and not a stereotype or an image.

—LORETTA LYNCH

'm not easily intimidated. Long ago, I realized that we are all on this journey together; we just play different roles. Realizing that helped me to understand that people are people. We all have hopes and dreams, fears and regrets, problems and solutions. Everyone brings a unique set of talents to the table and come of them what may. I have tremendous respect for people, especially those who have achieved notable positions. I admire many of them. I have tried to follow some of them. I am not, however, intimidated by them.

That changed the day that I met the attorney general of the United States. In a small conference room in the Central District of the Baltimore Police Department, I shook hands and had a meeting with Attorney General Loretta Lynch. In my life, I have never met a person who could seemingly see through your soul. I towered over her physically, yet her eyes pierced me in a way that was uncomfortable, revealing, and yes—intimidating.

Within fifteen seconds of talking with her, it was clear she got it, from both sides. She saw a police department that was battered and broken and a community awash in grief and despair. Even those who cared little about the abusive history of the BPD were traumatized by the sight of their city in flames. She made it clear, in language I was unaccustomed to from any politician, that she understood. In a bizarre way, I felt like a small child being comforted by a nurturing parent. She was going to make everything OK. Of course, intellectually I knew that we were far from being OK. Yet, as she headed back to her armored SUV, that was the feeling she had left in the room. It was going to be a long road to fix the problems. It wouldn't be easy. There would be missteps and failures along the way. But we knew she was going to work with us to make it right again. Finally, someone had heard the cry of those who so desperately wanted to bring reform into reality.

I didn't know at the time that a mere forty-five days later, I would no longer be a part of the process. In that moment, my only concern was trying to find a way to start putting the pieces back together again. I had tremendous hope that with the resources of the federal government behind us, all of those hopes I shared with Commissioner Batts could finally become a reality. We were going to reform the organization; we were going to better connect with our community; we were not going to allow the horrific tragedy that had just played out to be the final note of this mission. The universe had a different plan for me.

Three years later, my heart is still heavy. The reform effort in the BPD has been staggered. Officers are still being arrested. Command staff have been suspended for committing crimes. A Police commissioner has been federally indicted. And three years running, young black men in Baltimore continue to die at an unprecedented pace in a brutal and unending drug and gang war. It wears on my soul when I think of the lives lost and potential snuffed out. I cringe at the thought of another generation of Baltimoreans growing up with hatred and distrust in their hearts when they see police officers. I feel devastated when I think of the honorable and incredible women and men of the BPD who come into work every day trying to do their bit of good, against incredible odds, from inside and outside the department. I also know that there is a group of talented and dedicated people inside the department who are working to make things better. I pray that they succeed in their mission. The officers deserve it, and so does everyone who calls Baltimore home, myself included.

I never could have imagined having the adventure I embarked on three years ago. I got married to the most amazing man in the world. He serves our country proudly as a soldier, and I admire him more than words can ever convey. I have met amazing people across this great country: chefs and waiters, flight attendants, hotel employees, gas station attendants, doctors and nurses, elected officials in dozens of states, retail workers, lawyers, counselors, and students. In short, the American public. I've learned so much about what makes America what it is— how people of diverse backgrounds form their worldviews. I've listened to their experiences with law enforcement and shared my own. I've heard their support and admonishment, praise and criticism. The diversity of opinion is as mixed as the people who have offered them. Through it all, I have been filled with a sense of hope. I think everyone should travel the country. I think they would see the same sense of hope that I have found. Through all of the mundane trivialities of life, there is an overwhelming, shared sense of hope: the idea that this country will continue to move forward. That we will grow better and stronger as a nation. That as we learn and fix the mistakes of the past, we will make new ones, only to learn from those. It is a beautiful, almost tangible sense of optimism of what is to come.

I've also seen fear. Fear in the eyes of police officers in small towns and major cities. Fear that the good work they are doing is being ignored. That they are being judged not for their actions, but for the systemic issues that plague the law enforcement profession today. I've seen fear that they may not go home at night, simply because of the uniform they are wearing. It motivates me to push harder each day to do all I can to help. It means I'll get on another plane, in another airport, and stay at another hotel, missing my husband and home, if it means we can make a difference in one more town, one more city, one more life. The officers I've been blessed to meet are dedicated, hard-working, committed individuals who also hope for a time when they don't feel under siege. They, too, know the work that must be done to move forward.

I don't have all the answers. No one does, and as I've said before, anyone who says they do shouldn't be trusted. I do know there is a better way. It's one that I've spent the last three years teaching, and pushing, and advocating for. From rooms filled with more than 150 officers to small conference rooms with a mayor or city councilperson, I've shared my story and my vision. I hear from former students all the time who are amazed when they try something I've suggested and see it work. That motivates me as well. There is indeed hope that we will get to a better place.

I never envisioned writing a book. Even now, all these chapters in, it still feels a bit egotistical. Who am I to tell anyone what to do? Faith guides me, and my belief that we are all called to live our full potential demands that I do my very best each day. I'll continue to travel the country and do what I can. What I realized about six months ago was that this message needed to be heard far and wide. That it isn't just enough to talk to police officers and elected officials. We all must be in this together. Every person in this country has a role to play in what the future of policing looks like in this country. If, as a country, we are content to allow the status quo to continue to play out, then so be it. I don't think that's the case. My experience tells me that's not the case. The news stories I see every day tell me that's not the case. The continued human cry of despair in so many communities of color tells me that's not the case.

I've laid out the history of why we are here and the vision of how to move beyond our current daily existence. I'll continue to play my part. The question is, will you? Become a part of the process. Go to your local police department. Learn who they are. Connect with your city leaders and demand a different path. Work with legislators across the country to enact new and better laws that change the system for the better. Time and again, the history of this country shows us that when a group of people unite behind common ideals, great things can happen. We ended slavery because we saw the wrongs. We enacted civil rights because it was the right thing to do. We put a man on the moon because our destiny depended on it. We can fix this issue because the future of our children, especially those in our most disadvantaged communities, depends on it. Mostly, though, you don't know when your son or daughter, brother or sister, family member or friend, might be the next name on the ever-growing list of those whose deaths come at the hand of the systematic failures of law enforcement.

Please, hear my cry.

ACKNOWLEDGMENTS

I t's a daunting concept, trying to figure out how to thank all the people who helped this book become a reality. I drew on a lifetime of lessons, experiences, mentors, and leaders both good and bad, to give life to the words in my head. There is no way to appropriately thank all those who guided and shaped the person that I am today. I've always believed that we enter and exit from peoples' lives for reasons, to learn lessons, to grow, to become better people. To all those who played a role in shaping the person that I am today, you have my enduring thanks. If you helped me experience pain or joy, happiness or sorrow, stood as an obstacle or a offered a helping hand, I am who I am because of the lessons I learned (or had to learn a few times) because of those interactions. I wouldn't change a thing.

Having said that, there are a few people I need to thank specifically who played a pivotal role in this book coming into existence, starting with my incredible husband Jeff. He stood by me in my darkest days and supported this project in ways few will understand. A lifetime of happiness will only scratch at the surface of the debt I owe. I look forward to all the days to come.

My mother is probably the most amazing person I know. Her wit, her compassion, her love is without equal. Few people can make me laugh, smile, or share my insanity the way she can. She built the foundation of the man I am today. What greater gift is there than that?

Danny Scott and Bonnie Pugh are my family in ways that transcend words. Their quiet strength and encouragement helped me push forward, even when the task seemed too hard. If a man is judged by those in his life, I am lucky beyond words indeed.

The voices of Judy Pal and Lissa Druss paved a path of sanity for me in the worst of days. It is their friendship I treasure to this day. The three of us live a life centered around words. We relish in them. For all their help and assistance, I have two simple ones: thank you.

The world will never truly know the sacrifices Anthony Batts and Melissa Hyatt made for the people of Baltimore, not for their own glory, but for the protection of others. For the insight and guidance they provided me then and now, they have my thanks.

Finally, I am forever in debt to the Indie Books International team. From concept, to editing, to design, this process has been incredible. Writing a book is a massive undertaking. The entire team has made me feel like a part of a family I never knew I was missing. They have my utmost gratitude.

ABOUT THE AUTHOR

Eric Kowalczyk has developed a national reputation as a dynamic and engaging public speaker. Specializing in crisis communication and leadership strategies, Eric draws on a vast background of real-world and teaching experience to bring a new modality of communicating to varied professional audiences. In addition to his role as a public speaker and educator, he works with clients specializing in critical incident mitigation, strategy development for crisis resolution, crisis communications, public affairs, municipal communications, internal/external communications strategy, and media relations/training.

Eric has trained more than 1,000 communications specialists in forty states and sixty-five cities across the country. He has presented at numerous national conferences and is a 2016 TedXBeaconStreet speaker.

Handling local, national, and international media, Eric focused on transparency and accountability to connect with an already distrustful public during the Freddie Gray riots in Baltimore. Drawing from lessons learned during the Ferguson riots, Eric implemented and carried out a plan that was widely praised by media across the county as being responsive and understanding of community concerns.

Raised in New England, Eric is an avid football fan; he is also a devotee of philosophical studies, history, and music.

WORKS REFERENCED

"Ambush Killings of Police Officers Has Hit a 10-year High." *The Washington Post.* November 21, 2016. Accessed August 29, 2018. https://www.washingtonpost.com/news/wonk/wp/2016/11/21/ambush-killings-of-police-officers-has-hit-a-10-year-high/?utm_term=.1afeed9f5e6d. Baltimore Police Department. 2015 Civil Unrest: Looking Back—Moving Forward. Report. 2015.

Asmundson, Gordon J. G., and Jennifer A. Stapleton. "Associations Between Dimensions of Anxiety Sensitivity and PTSD Symptom Clusters in Active□Duty Police Officers." *Cognitive Behaviour Therapy* 37, no. 2 (2008): 66-75. doi:10.1080/16506070801969005.

Baltimore Police Department. 2015 *Civil Unrest: Looking Back—Moving Forward.* Report. 2015.

Braga, A. "The Effects of Hot Spots Policing on Crime." *The Annals of the American Academy of Political and Social Science* 578 (2012). doi:10.4073/csr.2012.8.

"BREAKING: Baltimore PD Confirms IED In Monday's Riots." Truth Revolt. April 29, 2015. Accessed September 10, 2018. https://www.truthrevolt.org/news/breaking-baltimore-pd-confirms-ied-mondays-riots.

Brown v. Board of Education of Topeka (1954).

Butler Center for Research. "Alcohol Abuse Among Police Officers." Jellinek Curve of Addiction | Hazelden Betty Ford Foundation. Accessed September 02, 2018. https://www.

hazeldenbettyford.org/education/bcr/addiction-research/
alcohol-abuse-police-ru-716.

"Bureau of Justice Statistics Home Page." Bureau of Justice
Statistics (BJS). Accessed September 10, 2018. https://www.
bjs.gov/index.cfm?ty=kfdetail&iid=493.

"Criminal Justice Fact Sheet." NAACP. Accessed August 30,
2018. http://www.naacp.org/criminal-justice-fact-sheet/.

"CNN's Harry Houck Speculates 'Some Right-Wing Group'
Could Be San Bernardino Shooters." NewsBusters. Accessed
September 10, 2018. https://www.newsbusters.org/blogs/
nb/curtis-houck/2015/12/02/cnns-harry-houck-speculates-
some-right-wing-group-could-be-san.

"Document: Indictment against Seven Baltimore Police
Officers." Baltimoresun.com. March 01, 2017. Accessed
September 10, 2018. http://www.baltimoresun.com/news/
maryland/crime/bal-document-indictment-against-seven-
baltimore-police-officers-20170301-htmlstory.html.

Final Report of the President's Task Force on 21st Century
Policing. Washington, D.C.: U.S. Department of Justice,
Office of Community Oriented Policing Services, 2015.

Goldberg, Bernard. *Bias: A CBS Insider Exposes How the Media
Distorts the News*. S.l.: Perennial, 2003.

Hadden, Sally E. *Slave Patrols: Law and Violence in Virginia
and the Carolinas*. Harvard University Press, 2003.

"History of Lynchings." NAACP. Accessed September 10, 2018.
https://www.naacp.org/history-of-lynchings/.

James, Erwin. "'Prison Is Not for Punishment in Sweden. We
Get People into Better Shape' | Erwin James." *The Guardian*.

November 26, 2014. Accessed September 10, 2018. https://www.theguardian.com/society/2014/nov/26/prison-sweden-not-punishment-nils-oberg.

Karam, Elie G., Matthew J. Friedman, Eric D. Hill, Ronald C. Kessler, Katie A. Mclaughlin, Maria Petukhova, Laura Sampson, Victoria Shahly, Matthias C. Angermeyer, Evelyn J. Bromet, Giovanni De Girolamo, Ron De Graaf, Koen Demyttenaere, Finola Ferry, Silvia E. Florescu, Josep Maria Haro, Yanling He, Aimee N. Karam, Norito Kawakami, Viviane Kovess-Masfety, María Elena Medina-Mora, Mark A. Oakley Browne, José A. Posada-Villa, Arieh Y. Shalev, Dan J. Stein, Maria Carmen Viana, Zahari Zarkov, and Karestan C. Koenen. "Cumulative Traumas And Risk Thresholds: 12-Month Ptsd In The World Mental Health (WMH) Surveys." *Depression and Anxiety* 31, no. 2 (2013): 130-42. doi:10.1002/da.22169.

Langton, Durose. U.S. Department of Justice Office of Justice Programs Bureau of Justice Statistics rev 2016

Loving v. Virginia (1967)

Lutz, Ashley. "These 6 Corporations Control 90% Of The Media In America." *Business Insider*. June 14, 2012. https://www.businessinsider.com/these-6-corporations-control-90-of-the-media-in-america-2012-6.

"Lynching in America: Confronting the Legacy of Racial Terror." Equal Justice Initiative. Accessed August 29, 2018. https://eji.org/reports/lynching-in-america.

"NAMI." National Alliance on Mental Illness. Accessed September 02, 2018. http://www.nami.org/Find-Support/Law-Enforcement-Officers.

Nittle, Nadra Kareem. "Understanding Jim Crow Laws." ThoughtCo. Accessed January 27, 2018. https://www. thoughtco.com/what-is-the-definition-of-jim-crow-laws-2834618.

O'Hara, Andy. "It's Time We Talk About Police Suicide." The Marshall Project. June 04, 2018. Accessed September 02, 2018. https://www.themarshallproject.org/2017/10/03/it-s-time-we-talk-about-police-suicide.

Plessy v. Ferguson (1896).

Puente, Mark, and Algerina Perna. "Sun Investigates: Undue Force." *The Baltimore Sun.* Accessed August 30, 2018. http://data.baltimoresun.com/news/police-settlements/.

Rhodes, William, et al. "Federal Sentencing Disparity: 2005-2012." Bureau of Justice Statistics (BJS), 2015, www.bjs. gov/index.cfm?ty=pbdetail&iid=5432.

Sherman, Lawrence W., Catherine H. Milton, and Thomas V. Kelly. *Team Policing: Seven Case Studies.* Washington, D.C.: Police Foundation, 1973.

Sheriff: 'I Was Sick to My Stomach' After Being Told To Stand Down." CBS Baltimore. April 30, 2015. Accessed September 02, 2018. http://baltimore.cbslocal.com/2015/04/30/sheriff-michael-lewis-on-the-stand-down-orders-given-to-city-officers/.

The Independent Committee on Reentry and Employment, Report and Recommendations. Report. April 25, 2006. https://www. reentry.net/ny/search/download.128868.

U.S. Department of Justice, Census of State and Local Law Enforcement Agencies, 2008

Wagner, Peter, and Alison Walsh. "States of Incarceration: The Global Context 2016." *Mass Incarceration: The Whole Pie 2016* | Prison Policy Initiative. Accessed September 03, 2018. https://www.prisonpolicy.org/global/2016.html.

"Women in Law Enforcement." *Secret Service Duties, Past, Present, & Future.* Accessed September 02, 2018. http://www.criminaljusticeschoolinfo.com/women-law-enforcement.html.

Workman-Stark, Angela L. *Inclusive Policing from the Inside Out.* Cham: Springer International Publishing, 2018.

www.ingramcontent.com/pod-product-compliance
Lightning Source LLC
Chambersburg PA
CBHW031935190326
41519CB00007B/542